T0354412

Of Roots and Wings

Of Roots and Wings

A Memoir

WAI WAI MYAING

OF ROOTS AND WINGS
A MEMOIR

iUniverse books may be ordered through booksellers or by contacting:

iUniverse
1663 Liberty Drive
Bloomington, IN 47403
www.iuniverse.com
1-800-Authors (1-800-288-4677)

ISBN: 978-1-4917-7872-2 (sc)
ISBN: 978-1-4917-8287-3 (hc)
ISBN: 978-1-4917-7871-5 (e)

Library of Congress Control Number: 2015918513

Print information available on the last page.

iUniverse rev. date: 03/16/2016

Dedicated to my grandchildren, Chan, Nay
Nay, and Zahni, the apples of my eye

Chan at age four in
Ho Chi Minh City

Zahni at age two at
Amara and Wyn Soe Lin's
wedding in Yangon

Nay Thurein at age two at
Pattaya Beach in Thailand

Foreword

When Daw Wai Wai Myaing asked me whether I would write a foreword for her second book, *Of Roots and Wings,* I felt pleased. At the same time, I was hesitant, unsure whether I could do justice to what she had achieved. Then I asked myself, "Why not take the challenge and try to do something to contribute in a small way to a work written by a Myanmar woman of stature – a scholar, an academic, and a good storyteller?"

I first came to know Wai Wai Myaing, also known as Winnie Aye Maung to her friends and contemporaries, while I was doing my postgraduate work in the Department of Economics at Rangoon University. I was a lecturing tutor, earning a hundred kyats more than a tutor who earned a monthly emolument of two hundred kyats.

Wai Wai Myaing was one of the students in my class. She, her classmates, and her friends were bright, attentive, and charming; they graced the Rangoon University campus. After graduating from the university, Wai Wai went on to study at the London School of Economics and Political Science, popularly known as LSE – a world-famous learning centre once headed by Michael Oakeshott and, before him, Harold Laski.

Besides Wai Wai Myaing, I had the good fortune to meet and work as colleagues with her younger brothers U Kyaw Myaing and U Linn Myaing, the latter of whom became an ambassador to the United States of America. I must not fail to mention Wai Wai Myaing's husband, U Soe Myint, who was a colleague of mine with the Foreign Service. U Soe Myint is a no-nonsense man who does not tolerate unfairness. I admire him for his intellect and pluck.

Daw Wai Wai Myaing has described her narrative as her "family story." In fact, she has portrayed Myanmar society, culture, and mores in a delightful way. In this book the reader also gets a bird's-eye view of Myanmar political transitions post-independence. With a touch of envy and much admiration, I do not hesitate to say that the book is a good read.

Tin Kyaw Hlaing
Foreign Service (retired)
February 2015

Author's Preface

This, my second book about my family's story, continues from where I left off in *A Journey in Time* with the college days of my parents, the Second World War, and how my parents fled the Myanmar capital city of Yangon to take shelter from the Allied and Japanese bombs in the villages near Hinthada. They returned to the city, with the Allied reoccupation of the country, to find their family home in Kyimyindine had been torched to the ground by British forces at the beginning of the war. They all took shelter in the *zayat* of the Bagaya Tawya Monastery on U Wisara Road, the zayat which my grandparents had built and donated in 1917. Four or five families lived there for as many years until civilian authority was re-established in the country. Once the country's administrative machine commenced to function, these people were taken back into their old jobs and professions and were availed of appropriate housing.

A discerning reader who has continued to be interested in my family's story would notice the pace of the narrative quickening as independence was granted to the former British colony. Almost immediately, widespread insurrection erupted as major players in the fight against colonialism demanded their right to govern the country according to their own political beliefs and faiths. This was a newly minted country, war ravaged though it might be, and they wanted to see it tread the path of their choosing.

So the tale which can have no ending unfolds as future generations of our family take the places of the ones preceding them. But, thankfully, I can take ownership of the recording of only a small stretch of this road. To be precise, my narrative ends in 2008, an arbitrary point in our family's history. I have tried my hardest to make this book truthful, acceptable to the people who appear in it, and factually accurate as to events that took place.

One phenomenon surfaced and engaged my interest as I wrote this perhaps very personal account of my family and the times we inhabited it. It is referred to quite transparently in the title of the book: *Of Roots and Wings.* It amuses me to think that if my granddaughter, at the cocky age of eleven (in 2011), were to know of this choice of title, she would call it "corny." However, that is what I have tried to understand: the way my family, among with many others in our country, have scattered around the world in this age of so-called globalization. Have we or our children maintained the Myanmar values, traditions, and culture that had been such a rich part of our parents' and grandparents' lives? Is it fair of us to expect our children, and their children, to uphold these things in the lives they lead in times and lands very far away and very different? Or is it even an issue? And if not, should it be? In my heart of hearts, I think I may have an answer.

Wai Wai Myaing
Yangon, 2015

Acknowledgements

Tun Htut Myaing, my nephew who works and lives in New York, has patiently and obligingly taken time out from his busy life as artist and curator to humour his elder aunt (*kyee kyee*) and design the book cover. I had the idea and a vague form in my head, and he translated it into a beautiful romantic image, which I immediately recognized as the one I sought.

Another talented and obliging nephew, Tin Aung Myaing, who lives in Manhattan and works from his home office as a software architect, introduced me to a marvellous genealogy application. It can take in all the data I can gather of our Myaing clan reaching across eight generations and present the connections in (to me) an impressive variety of ways. I am, however, limited to using in this book a very simplified version, for obvious reasons.

Myo Htut Myaing, another nephew, recently returned from New Jersey and contributed his time and skills to install the database from which we produced the family trees of U Tha Myaing's seven offspring, shown in Appendix IV

My daughter, Wai Sann Thi, always supportive of my undertakings, did the tedious job of reading the draft. She was able to give me very refreshing as well as valuable direction for my final version. I trusted her instincts as if they were my own.

My son, Aung Thura, in spite of the tightest of work schedules and frequent travel, took enough time to facilitate a professional layout and design of the final version of the book.

I owe the most gratitude to my *Sayar,* U Tin Kyaw Hlaing, who courageously undertook the task of introducing a little-known author on the strength of having had her as a student during her college days. I have, however, known him subsequently as my husband's colleague in the Ministry of Foreign Affairs, which tenure culminated in his ambassadorship to Nepal and, later, in his appointment as ambassador, permanent representative, to the United Nations Office at Geneva. My brothers Kyaw Myaing and Linn Myaing both had the privilege of working for a very experienced and skilled diplomat of the old school in Ambassador Tin Kyaw Hlaing.

My friends from way back when added colour and texture to this simple narrative.

Last, I owe the inspiration and the raison d'être for this book to my immediate and extended family, on whom I have in part based the story and for whom I have undertaken the task, albeit without their asking. It was a task which I have found to be of immense satisfaction and meaning to me.

List of Acronyms

ABAC, Assumption Business Administration College (Assumption University of Thailand)

AFO, Anti-Fascist Organization

AFPFL, Anti-Fascist People's Freedom League

AIIMS, All India Institute of Medical Sciences

ASEAN, Association of Southeast Asian Nations

BAF, Burma Air Force

BAA, Burma Athletic Association

BBC, British Broadcasting Corporation

BIA, Burma Independence Army

BNA, Burma National Army

BOAC, British Overseas Airways Corporation

BSPP, Burma Socialist Programme Party

CBD, Central Business District

CUNY, City University of New York

DSA, Defence Services Academy

DSMA, Defence Services Medical Academy

DSTA, Defence Services Technical Academy

ESCAP, Economic and Social Council for Asia and the Pacific

FAO, Food and Agricultural Organization

GCE, General Certificate of Education

ISM, International School Myanmar

ISY, International School Yangon (formerly ISR, International School Rangoon)

KNDO, Karen National Defence Organization

MEHS, Methodist English High School

MEHSA, Methodist English High School Alumni

MEOSA, Methodist English Old Students' Association

MEP, *Missions Etrangéres de Paris*

MOFA, Ministry of Foreign Affairs

NCWB, National Council of Women in Burma

OBE, Order of the British Empire

PBF, Patriotic Burmese Forces

PVO, People's Volunteer Organization

RAF, Royal Air Force

RUBC, Rangoon University Boat Club

SHS, State High School

SLORC, State Law and Order Restoration Council

TTC, Teacher Training College

UBA, Union of Burma Airways

UNDP, United Nations Development Programme

UNESCO, United Nations Economic, Social, and Cultural Organization

UNGA, United Nations General Assembly

UNTAC, United Nations Transitional Authority in Cambodia

UNTAET, United Nations Transitional Authority in East Timor

UTC, University Training Corps

VOA, Voice of America

Table of Contents

Of Roots and Wings (1969–2005)

A Wider World (2000–08)

Part I

A Legacy of Love
(1948-68)

Chapter 1

Freedom at Dawn

In the dim, early hours of a cool winter's day, a line of official cars snaked its way out of the governor's residence on Windsor Road, Rangoon. Elsewhere, citizens of the city tramped to the site downtown, talking exuberantly or in contained excitement, to witness an event which they would remember for the rest of their lives.

I was nine when Burma regained its independence, on 4 January 1948. A formal ceremony was held at exactly 4.20 a.m., a time deemed to be the most astrologically auspicious for such an important event, at what became known as Independence Square (now known as Maha Bandoola Park after the most famous Burmese general of the nineteenth century) in downtown Rangoon. The ceremony was witnessed by the British governor Sir Hubert Rance and his staff; President-elect Sao Shwe Thaik; Burmese ministers and senior officials; and invited guests. Jubilant crowds, who had waited for this moment as they celebrated privately throughout the night, made their way to witness the ceremony in the cool, misty morning. Now with the Burmese flag raised aloft, cheering and shouting were heard, and rifles were fired in the air. For the many Burmese who had lived under years of foreign occupation, it was a day they had hardly dared to hope for after long years of struggle and patient submission. Children, of our generation, caught the heady excitement of the significance of the day that would stay with us for the remainder of our lives.

The handing over of government was done in a formal ceremony at half past seven that morning at the old governor's residence. The Union Jack was lowered, and the Burmese flag was hoisted to take its place. The newly formed cabinet filed in and were sworn in, pledging their loyalty to the first president of the Republic of Burma. This was followed by a march-past of the British armed forces: the British Army, the Royal Navy, and the Royal Air Force followed by the newly formed Burma army led by a contingent of the Burma navy, army, and air force, in that order. This was the first and last time the naval arm was given precedence over the army in any such formal occasion.

A breakfast party followed this, but the president and the prime minister, and most of the latter's ministers, rushed off to the jetty to wave goodbye to Governor and Lady Rance as they embarked on HMS *Birmingham.* The two national anthems were again played, and a twenty-one-gun salute was fired, in honour of the new republic.

Celebrations on that day included a cruise down the Kandawgyi, translated as Royal Lakes, by the new president and his entourage in a royal barge specially constructed for the event. There were boat races watched by crowds lined along the Kandawgyi's banks as a traditional Myanmar orchestra provided rousing music. Later and less formal occasions included the navy dance held at the Orient Club attended by the newly appointed commander-in-chief of the Burma navy, Commander Kin Maung Bo.

All over Burma, in big cities and small towns, this scene was replicated. The Union Jack was brought down, and the six-star-studded Burmese flag was hoisted to the top of the pole. In far-off Mogok, as retold by a cousin, everyone was happy and in high spirits. On the appointed day, at the appointed time, the senior British resident of Mogok, a gems merchant by the name of A. C. D. Pain, lowered the Union Jack. That night, the small town reverberated with the sound of music from numerous *anyeint* and *zat* performances.

I remember the excitement of being asked to join the staff members' families at the main railways office on what is now Bogyoke Aung San Road, to witness the fireworks on the evening of 4 January, while my father and mother attended a special celebratory dinner at Government House hosted by Sao Shwe Thaike, the first president of independent Burma. It must have been a glittering and jubilant crowd at the presidential residence.

For those of us who were old enough to experience it, the exultation the Burmese people felt upon the gaining of our country's independence was a never-to-be-forgotten moment. Young as children of our age were, we felt from our elders the tremendous release of throwing off the yoke of nearly a century of hated servitude and bottled-up frustration. It was not so much that the colonial masters were universally an evil lot; maybe some were. The basic premise of colonialism certainly was, and so too the degradation and the frustration of being second-class citizens in one's own country. Younger generations who had not lived under a colonial master, or even experienced it second-hand from elders who had, could never appreciate the difference between living under foreign domination and living in independence. Undoubtedly, on a personal level, there were many friendships that were sincere as well as deep lasting, and many relationships invested with dignity, between members of the two races. In these cases, human decency prevailed. And where it did not, there were victims on both sides.

However that may be, independence for a country and its people is the most eventful and defining moment. Many were caught up in the euphoria and the exultation of the moment, tending to forget the responsibilities, and the burdens, associated with becoming one's own master. Burma's independence should have been like any coming of age, an event worthy of sombre reflection and taking stock. Our great leader Bogyoke Aung San exhorted to his people in his last ever public speech, in his usual blunt language, six days before his assassination on 13 July 1947:

> If you want independence, you need the discipline that will ensure it. If you want independence, you need to preserve the unity that is required for it. If you want independence you

5

need to work on the reconstruction of the country that will bring it about. If, afterward, you want to enjoy the fruits of independence you need to work hard, to be disciplined and get rid of old habits, bad habits and worthless habits. That is what I want to say to you today.

Independence Day celebrations in New Delhi, India,
hosted by Burmese Ambassador H. E. U Win and attended by
Lord and Lady Mountbatten (Lord Mountbatten was governor
general of India at the time), 4 January 1948

(Courtesy of Daw Khin Khin Maw)

Hoisting of the six-star-studded Burmese Flag,
Independence Day, 4 January 1948

A traditional dance troupe performs for guests at the
Independence Day celebrations in New Delhi, India, 4 January 1948

Chapter 2

Insurrections

Less than a year into the young republic's independence, in 1948, Burma's freely elected government under U Nu was faced with insurgency from the breakaway communist ideologists. In fact, newly independent Burma was challenged by a multitude of problems. The Red Flag Communist Party under Thakin Soe had refused to compromise in any way with the British during the pre-independence talks. The White Flag Communist Party under Thakin Than Tun, a one-time comrade of Bogyoke Aung San in their fight for independence, held that the Anti-Fascist People's Freedom League (AFPFL) had sold the country short to the imperialists and openly opposed U Nu. Incredibly, Than Tun addressed a mass meeting in Bandoola Square in the centre of town and called for an armed uprising. At this, the government issued orders for the capture of the communist leadership, but this came too late, as those leaders had fled to the hills behind Pyinmana and made their base in the forests of the Bago Yomas. Inevitably, the Bago region became a hotbed of communist activity. The communists dug out the arms and ammunitions that had been cached there at the end of World War II. Using these, they terrorized the surrounding towns and villages, overran military outposts, and blew up railway lines and bridges. Because of these initial successes in open revolt against the government and because many people were susceptible to communist ideology and rhetoric, many people, including simple villagers, swelled the ranks of these parties.

When the communists went underground, the People's Volunteer Organization (PVO), made up of tens of thousands of ex-soldiers who had served under Aung San in the Burma National Army (BNA) and who had later been demobilized, began to waver. When U Nu laid out the leftist solidarity fifteen-point action plan, the PVOs split into two factions: the Yellow Flag PVOs and the White Flag PVOs. The Yellow Flag PVOs endorsed U Nu and the White Flag PVOs, under Bo La Yaung, a member of the Thirty Comrades, went underground in July 1948.

Also, late in 1948 Karen paramilitary formations were being quietly raised. The motivating forces were the distrust and the animosity that had been ignited since the war for Burma's independence. The Karen National Defence Organization, or the KNDO, started open rebellion about this time.

After the world war and with the reoccupation of Burma by the British, the fate of the BNA, with its thousands of rank and file, had to be decided. On 6 and 7 September 1945 in the highland town of Kandy, Ceylon, a meeting was held between the Allied supreme commander Lord Mountbatten and Major General Aung San, the latter as leader of the newly titled Patriotic Burmese Forces (PBF). They drew up a plan called the Kandy Agreement. According to this agreement, a new Burma army was to be formed with two hundred former PBF officers and fifty-two hundred of the PBF's rank-and-file members. These soldiers were assigned to the 3rd, 4th, and 5th Burma Rifles and to the artillery regiment at Meiktila. Officers received the king's commission and thus became officers owing allegiance to King George VI of England. It was an ironic fact that Burmese officers who had trained under the Japanese, and who upon returning to Burma after the end of the war were imprisoned for having done so, were now given the king's commission and given training under the British. But for these officers, their loyalty never wavered; it was all part of their continuing fight for independence. [1] The new Burma army also consisted of three Karen battalions, known as the 1st, 2nd,

---

[1] Bohmhugyi Tin Maung (retd.) *Taing pyay ka nu nu monhtine ka htan htan* (Yangon,1973)

and 3rd Karen Rifles battalions; two Kachin battalions; and two Chin battalions mainly made up of members of the British Army during the Japanese campaign. "It was intended to represent and unite various (political) groups in Burma, but in fact, it had detrimental consequences ... was an unfavourable joining together of two antagonistic groups: BNA/PBF veterans, mostly Burmans, and Karen, Kachin and Chin ethnic minorities 'class units' that had remained loyal to the Allies."[2]

Marxist ideology had preceded anti-fascism in the resistance movement, so it was not surprising that the Burma army inherited many who had leftist leanings. Now with open rebellion from the communists and the White Flag PVOs, many in the army sympathetic to these groups felt that the time was ripe to bring about political change by force of arms. Whole units of the army went underground. The 1st Burma Rifles went underground. More than half of the 3rd Burma Rifles, led by Lt. Colonel Ye Htut, did the same. Thus, left holding the Union of Burma flag was half of the 3rd, the 4th, the 5th, and the 6th Burma Rifles, the last of which was newly formed. The others were the 2nd Burma Rifles, consisting mostly of Karen and other nationalities; the 1st, 2nd, and 3rd Chin Rifles; the 1st and 2nd Kachin Rifles; the 1st, 2nd, and 3rd Karen Rifles; and the 4th Infantry made up of Gurkha soldiers. However, with the open rebellion of the KNDO, the continued loyalty of the Karen forces in the army became seriously in doubt. For these forces, which were already garrisoned in particular towns, it was a matter of declaring whose side they were on and then capturing the town in that faction's name.

Along the Rangoon–Mandalay railroad and in Myingyan, Mandalay, and Toungoo, the only army units stationed were Karen. In January 1949, the inevitable happened: the 1st Karen Rifles defected to join forces with the KNDO and then occupied Toungoo. In Pyinmana, Kachin forces under Naw Seng, the anti-Japanese war hero, went underground and marched towards Meiktila. The defence of Meiktila was carried out with a few units of volunteers and people's militia who were neither properly trained nor organized. Meiktila

---

[2] Myoma Lwin, *The Gun That Saved Rangoon* (Oxfordshire, 2011)

soon fell, losing several officers and men. Soon afterwards, Maymyo fell to enemy hands in a bizarre turn of events. The Union of Burma Airways (UBA) passenger plane that flew into enemy territory unknowingly in Meiktila on the day that it was taken was commandeered by Boh Naw Seng and was taken to AniSakhan, the airfield that served Maymyo. The troops guarding the airfield had no inkling that these were enemy forces until the former were disarmed. Naw Seng then drove into the town and, having contacted the Karen units there, occupied it without having to fire a shot.

On 1 February 1949, Insein was taken by Karen forces that were massed in that area. Within a few days, the 2nd Karen Rifles occupied Prome. A strategy was forged to mount a two-pronged attack by two Karen rebel forces, one from Toungoo and the other from Prome, to consolidate and march down to attack Rangoon. A last-minute defence was mounted at Wetkaw on the highway that leads from Rangoon to Prome. A Burma navy Bofors gun was to provide artillery support for three of the four companies of the 3rd Burifs as they faced the 2nd Karen Rifles battalion, "the most powerful, professional and experienced unit of the Burma Army."[3] If that attack had succeeded, a completely different history might have been written for Burma. Lt Kyaw Thein Lwin, the naval officer who had commanded the artillery unit, detailed the successful defence of Wetkaw in his book *The Gun That Saved Rangoon.*

In the darkest hours of the insurrection, government forces had retreated to Sagaing after the fall of Mandalay, which came soon after the fall of Maymyo. In the south, in the delta regions, the 3rd and 4th Burma Rifles held on to a few key towns. The rest were in enemy hands. Parts of the 3rd Rifles were engaged in Hmawbi. Surrounding them were hundreds of KNDOs and thousands of communists. The 5th Burma Rifles and some Chin troops were bitterly fighting in Insein. What was left of the 6th Burma Rifles engaged the enemy in the Bago front.

Thus, all along the railway line from Mandalay to Nyaunglebin was KNDO territory, with a pocket of defence by government forces in Thazi. The KNDOs and communists

---

[3] Ibid.

had gained control in most of the delta towns. Right on the doorstep of the government capital Rangoon, a mere eight miles away, Insein had fallen to enemy hands. Except for a few major towns, the Moulmein–Thaton region was also in KNDO control. Along the Irrawaddy, in towns like Yenangyaung, Magwe, Minbu, and Prome, there were communists, PVOs, and rebel army units. The young army held on with its depleted forces and depleted arms and ammunitions with the help of volunteers and militia, who were untrained and inexperienced, often fighting against the trained army units of the segments that had defected. Officers who had attended training together under the British in Meiktila were now facing each other across enemy lines. Many were the times when the enemy had called upon the defending government factions to surrender, citing superior numbers, but officers and men hung on grimly in the face of dwindling numbers of men, dwindling resources, and dwindling ammunition.

My family were in a Burma Railways quarter in Hume Road when Karen forces seized Insein, just nine miles away from the heart of the city. It was said that their scratch forces penetrated to within four miles of it. Panic and confusion reigned. Whole families fled to safer parts of the city and were given accommodation in refugee centres like the one in a big building near the Prome Road Railway Station. Machine-gun fire and mortar shells were heard throughout the city; I was terrified by the ominously close gunfire. We were too young to understand the terror of the Japanese and Allied bombs during World War II while we sheltered in the underground bunkers, but we were certainly old enough now to appreciate the danger of the machine-gun fire. Sandbags were piled in the ground floor; we were supposed to take cover behind these. Other than that, we just had to pray that the defending government forces would be able to drive the insurgents out. Thankfully, within two weeks of this onslaught the insurgents were driven back to Insein. And within four months, the Karen positions at the seminary, the railway workshops, and the veterinary college in Insein were wrested from them and they retreated across the Hlaing River. Life returned to normal in

Rangoon. But the insurgency raged on, at times fiercely, other times at low key, but it was never extinguished in remote parts of the country.

The government was certainly beset and encircled by gravely problematic factions challenging its authority. In a book entitled *Taing pyay ka nu nu mon htine ka htan htan* Bohmhugyi Tin Maung (retd) portrays the magnitude of the problems facing the young republic. It is illuminating to read the list of towns captured by the various rebels in 1949 in Hugh Tinker's *The Union of Burma: A Study of the First Years of Independence.* That list is provided below.

KNDO

1. Bassein (25–29 January 1949)
2. Insein (31 January–22 May 1949)
3. Twante (1 January–13 June 1949)
4. Pantanaw (? April 1949–25 February 1950)
5. Einme (1 February 1949–11 November 1950)
6. Nyaunglebin (20 April 1949–25 February 1950)
7. Toungoo (25 January 1949–19 March 1950)
8. Meiktila (20 February–23 March 1949)
9. Kyaukse (with communists; 21 February–26 June 1949)
10. Maymyo (21 February–17 April 1949)
11. Mandalay (with communists; 13 March–24 April 1949)
12. Loikaw (? February 1949–12 January 1950)
13. Taunggyi (13 August–23 November 1949)
14. Lashio (27 August 1949)
15. Namkhan (31 August–8 September 1949)

Communists

16. Henzada (with PVO;? March–27 August 1949)
17. Tharawaddy (9 April–27 August 1949)
18. Pyinmana (20 February 1949–29 March 1950)
19. Yamethin (20 February–? March 1949)
20. Myingyan (23 February–10 July 1949)
21. Pakokku (? March 1949–29 April 1950)

PVO and Army Mutineers

22. Prome (9 August–9 September 1948, and 1 February 1949–19 May 1950)
23. Thayetmyo (8–30 August 1948, and 17 March 1949–5 October 1950)
24. Magwe (25 February 1949–8 April 1950)
25. Minbu (25 February 1949–8 April 1950)
26. Yenangyaug (23 February–10 June 1949)
27. Chauk (23 February–? June 1949)
28. Sandoway (10 June 1949–27 October 1950)
29. Kyaukpyu (10 June–15 July 1949)

Mujahids

30. Rathedaung (with communists; 1 January–4 February 1950)
31. Buthidaung (1 January–4 February 1950)

By November 1949, initiative had passed to the government forces, who retook one town after another. By the end of 1951, the rebels no longer were a threat to the existence of the State. But at the height of the insurgency, when the insurgents succeeded in closing in on the government right up to its capital, the government was called the "Rangoon government," implying that it had control over only its capital – while the multicoloured insurgents controlled the rest of the country. All economic and social progress in the country had to be subordinated to the military struggle, certainly until 1952. And U Nu's vision for Burma as a "welfare state" was put on hold.

Many times in the 1950s, my father, a traffic manager at the time, was summoned to inspect and make repairs at places on the railway line which had been wrecked by one band or another of the insurgents. Trains were derailed and passengers were killed, leading to disrupted railway traffic for days or weeks. It was a favourite tactic of the insurgents to disrupt communications on the main railway line joining the northern part of the country to its capital. It was not considered safe to travel around the country beyond a certain distance, and business people and others who did so out of necessity did so at their peril, for buses and trains were often ambushed and passengers robbed and kidnapped.

After the Karen insurgency threat to the capital passed, our days in Rangoon were pleasant enough, spent between school and home. School was always fun. Lessons were not so difficult. Our intelligence grew in pace with our learning, and our parents never put pressure on us to get the top positions in class. They never minded that we did not. They never had to help us with our homework, although I remember that we often asked the help of our cousins who were staying with us in Rangoon while they attended college. We passed our courses comfortably every year.

At about this time, Ko Myaing, a cousin of ours living in Mogok, had a fateful meeting with U Chit Hlaing, an elder brother of one of his classmates. He succumbed to the brilliant oratory of the well-known ideologist who later became the brains behind "The Burmese Way to Socialism," and converted to communism. When the party was declared illegal, he went underground. At age fourteen, he had marched all the way to Mandalay. The rifle he carried towered a hand span above his head. After about two years, he was captured while trying to raise funds from family friends. After this, he was put into jail and charged with treason. He could have languished in prison for twenty years or for life if found guilty. The minister of education at that time was friendly with his father, our elder uncle U Tha Kyawt, who was an inspector of schools. The two men had worked together for a time at the Anti-Fascist Organization (AFO). A promise was extracted that our uncle's son would go back to school if released. At the next court hearing, my cousin was flown back to Rangoon. It was a measure of the minister's wisdom and leniency that a boy of sixteen was judged not by his youthful convictions but on his potential for future good. In hindsight, I see that my cousin's view, as is the case for many like him who followed ideologies, is that communism is for near saints and that in its implementation mere humans can only fall far short of its ideals.

Flush with the feelings of freedom and national independence, and with idealistic notions of repairing the evils of the past in their country, many young college students came under the influence of communist ideologies. Even though they did not go so far as to go underground, they did espouse their ideas in everyday dealings with people they come in contact with. Another cousin of ours for whom communism seemed like a fashion statement assumed a slightly superior air and an amused condescension about the fact that our family had domestic help in the form of cooks and maids. He went out of his way to be extra courteous to them, to make up for the social stratification that was abhorrent to him. While we were used to taking our domestics' services for granted and treating them with normal courtesy, he went to great pains to refuse being served and to address them using honorific names. He would then lecture us younger cousins on the evils of exploitation, which idea wafted way over our heads. He was to us hardly credible as a communist, being the scion of a long line of landlords on his mother's side. He was a charming and lovable cousin and quite the beau among a bevy of girls his age. We who had not had the benefit of taking college courses in philosophy and sociology or of reading Marxist ideology just used our everyday experiences to parry with him. He would just laugh at us good-naturedly, as if to say, "You are too young to know better." We would then let him march us all off amiably to Daw Nu Aung's Ice Cream Parlour, which was conveniently located near our house on Prome Road. There we forgot all our dissent about isms and ideologies. In fact, one of our other cousins remembered that Ko Win's visits always meant an ice cream treat for us younger cousins.

Map showing the territories occupied by various insurgents in 1949
(reproduced from *The Guardian, Rangoon*, of 27 March 1962)

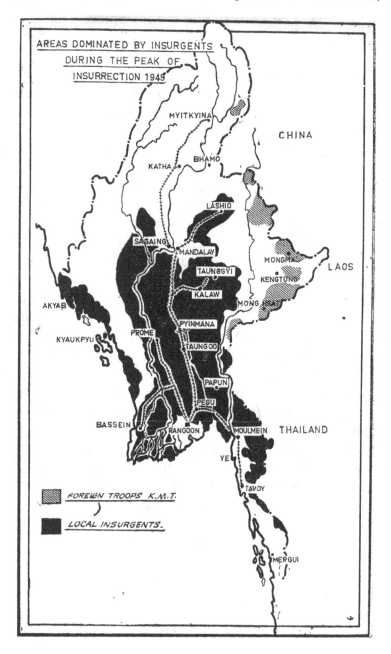

Chapter 3

Midnight Feasts and Fantasies

In the early 1950s, when my brother Htut and I were in our pre-teens and our two younger siblings were just starting school, our family had a Ford van. Htut and I were a little more than a year apart. Moe and Polay had joined us much later, delayed by the exact span of the war years. The reason I remember the van so vividly is because our parents would, as a special treat, take us in it for a late-evening foray into Chinatown to eat at those

Wai Wai, Htin (Htut), Kyaw (Moe), and Linn Myaing (Po Lay) at ages eleven, ten, five, and three, respectively

little roadside shops which sell delicious noodles. Father would park the van by the curb, and someone from the shop would rush to run a plank of wood through one window and straight out the other, as a makeshift table. Then fragrant bowls of noodle soup or steamed duck noodles or roasted pork noodles would be served to us. A variation of these would be with wonton packets instead of noodles. There was also more exotic fare that the adults were more partial to. For us children, even this array proved a most difficult challenge, as we agonized over what to order.

Friends of an earlier generation remembered that the Indian quarter on Thompson Road had the same custom of running a plank through the car windows of its patrons. Then, a plate of crispy *paratha* was dumped onto the plank, with the purpose either to stem the tide of hunger or to whet the appetite for more lavish fare. Orders could be made for *keema paratha,* crispy layers of paratha stuffed with a spicy meat mixture, or goat-knuckle soup or spicy goat brain curry, to name a few of the more fancy items. For ice cream, people went to a little shop on the fourth floor of a tiny apartment building on Thirty-fourth Street. There, clients had a choice of strawberry, chocolate, vanilla, or coconut ice cream and the small steel cups were lowered from the fourth-floor window. One would think there would be insurmountable problems in having to sell ice cream from a fourth-floor apartment, but that hardly seemed the case. The business flourished as patrons came in a steady stream.

Sugar-cane juice from a Thompson Road shop was the talk of the town for decades. In the heat of the dry season, it was easy to entice others to join you to drive over to the Thompson Road shop. Parked by the roadside and by the glare of the fluorescent light, you could order frothy, pale green sugar-cane juice filled to the brim of thick, tall glasses. Little lumps of ice clinked invitingly in them. People of our generation and older, in their nostalgic ramblings, could describe the streets in town that had the best of a particular kind of a variety of specialty foods. They were connoisseurs, with the most expensive of currencies i.e. time at their disposal to seek out these places in each other's company.

Indian and Chinese, and sometimes Panthay/Nonya, were the main cuisines that people chose for their early evening meals or midnight suppers. The food and the enjoyment of it was paramount. People didn't put on airs or assume pretensions. Indeed, because it was so soon after the war and the subsequent destruction, there were no grand restaurants or hotels. Parents would take their young families, and adult children would take their ageing parents, out as a special treat. Friends would take each other out for the dual enjoyment of the company and the food.

We children enjoyed going out at what would normally be our bedtime to eat the delicious food. We also looked forward to the outings with great delight, because of the companionship we shared. Instead of sitting on the seats, we would ride into town lying on the mat which was laid on the floor of the luggage compartment of the car, giggling and making up games and stories. Alas, our imaginations were never too taxed because the trip into town was not such a long drive. We wished it were longer, but we were just as eager to clamber onto the seats in front and get ready to tuck into the food.

I could not remember the subject of our fantasy adventures, although I imagine they were probably mostly related to the tales of the Jataka, the five hundred lives of our lord Buddha in his previous existences before attaining Buddhahood. While *Lord of the Rings* or *Harry Potter* fired the imagination of our children's and grandchildren's generation, the Jataka tales were for us as rich in majesty and magic. What was more is that they were not mere adventures; the moral lessons and values imbued in all these tales were to last us a lifetime. Our grand-aunt, or whom we had always perceived to be our grand-aunt because she had always been with our family and taken care of us, told these to us. She was, in fact, a distant relative who had been in my mother's family since her mother's days. On weekends in the afternoons, when my parents were out with their friends playing golf or cards, Dwe (or Yay, as we called her, for some now-forgotten reason) would gather us around her on a mat, she lying in the middle and two of us on each side of her. She would read from a book or tell us these stories from memory, as they had most probably been told to her by her mother or aunts when she was small. These were all uplifting and inspiring stories, as they relate the virtues all we Buddhists aspire to: generosity, compassion, perseverance, understanding, and forbearance. For example, there was the tale of King Vesandara to inspire us to dizzying heights of generosity; the tale of Prince Janekha to show us the fruits of perseverance; the tale of the Monkey King to illustrate what forbearance could mean; and many, many others. We listened with wide-eyed wonder and were given the glimmerings of the heights of moral virtue we should aspire to.

Chapter 4

Illicit Tales

There were also all the illicit tales told to us out of the hearing of our parents or elders. These were told by our maids, who had come from the villages and were full of accounts of the custodian spirits of the treasure trove of pagodas, and of the witches, or *sone,* that haunt the remote little outhouses in the village clearing. They would appear as flickering lights that danced about in the gloaming. The custodian spirits of the pagodas, known as *ossasaunt,* were said to appear as beautiful, ethereal young maidens. Sometimes while visiting the terrestrial domain, one of them would fall in love with a human, a young, handsome woodcutter or a hunter, whom she would entice to join her in her world. Upon agreeing to do so, the young man would forfeit his life. Sometimes, ossasaunts were allowed to spend a certain portion of their spirit lives as humans, always promising to return to their original existence. In such a case, an ossasaunt would be born as a human and then invariably die as a spinster, her compatriots in the other existence not being in favour of her forming any mortal attachments. If she went against this rule and decided to marry, she would die suddenly and unexpectedly before this event could take place. This is seen as her being recalled to her world of ossasaunts for flouting the terms of the agreement that allowed her to spend some time in the human world. There were a few coincidental events among my family's close circle of relatives whose sudden deaths were thought to be linked to their having come from this extraterrestrial world.

There were also other spine-chilling stories. One of these spoke of a *mhaw sayar,* or an exorcist, who, upon finding out that a certain human came from the land of the ossasaunts, would use his powers to thrash and flog her in order to make her reveal the caches of gold and jewels that she had been guarding for the coming of the *Arreimedeya Buddha,* the fifth and last Buddha that will arise in what is known as the *Badda Kabar.* Our parents and aunts and uncles frowned upon these tales, however gripping and awesomely fascinating to us children they may have been, and reprimanded the maids for filling our heads with such melodrama. Our elders would not, however, deny the existence of ossasaunts, since in the Myanmar Buddhist hierarchy of existences there dwell a host of beings in a whole gamut of noble and ignoble lives. Our parents and other relatives just did not want our young minds to be unduly impressed with sensationalized renderings of what we Buddhists accept as coexisting beings. The same is true of the lurid ghost stories that our maids would tell us, most probably in a bid to keep us quiet and docile instead of wreaking havoc in the house, which they would have to deal with afterwards! We were told by our elders, who were always teaching us by words and example, that we did not need to be afraid of ghosts and spirits, that they coexist with us, albeit on a different plane, and all we are exhorted to do is to share our good deeds with them by distributing merit and sending them goodwill, or metta, in the hope that they soon be delivered from their lowly existence. But with us children being children, we loved to hear these tales in all their embellished forms. We relished the chills that went tingling up our spines. We felt, however, that, armed with the knowledge of the real nature of these ghosts and spirits, we knew how we should relate to them so they did not ever harm us.

Chapter 5

Vanishing Customs

Whenever my family visited our zayat in the early fifties, before *Pho Pho* (my maternal grandfather) became bedridden, we went back to a time when family customs still held sway. For example, there were the times when we would gather around to watch Pho Pho

Bagaya Tawya Zayat on U Wisara Road, built and donated by our grandparents in 1917

make beautiful paper lanterns at Thadingyut (Festival of Lights). He, dressed in a loose cotton jacket and *pasoe,* and with his long hair in a topknot, would sit on the floor of the zayat with a pile of bamboo saplings, which he thinned and smoothed with a thin, sharp knife. He would construct big stars or cylindrical shapes out of these saplings. Sheets of coloured cellophane would be cut to fit over these structures, making them into beautiful lanterns. In our house for the same Festival of Lights, we would just make do with candles or oil lamps strung out on windowsills and on verandah rails. Our father did not have the skill or the time to make paper lanterns. These days, even the lanterns have been replaced by electric bulbs, multicoloured and strung out in fancy shapes.

Once a week when we observed the Eight Precepts, which entailed fasting after the midday meal, Aunty Ngwe (Pho Pho's daughter) and Aunty Mya (Pho Pho's daughter-in-law) would always see to it that a special table was laid out for the sole meal of the day. Aunty Mya would make sure to buy a variety of meats, vegetables, fruits, and sweetmeats during her daily shopping at Myenigone Market. Aunty Ngwe would cook the meal with the help of other female members of the household, some peeling onions and pounding them together with chillies and garlic in a mortar, some cleaning and cutting the meat and fish, some preparing the vegetable dips with the all-important *ngapi-yay* – and each taking responsibility for a segment of the midday meal. Believe it or not, it took three or four people, in a sort of fraternal frenzy, the whole morning to do that without the help of any time-saving gadgets on a blazing wood fire.

In time, the table would be laid with an appetizing array of meat, fish, and vegetarian dishes to cater to the tastes of all the people who would be fasting, so that they might have a satisfactory meal to last them through the whole day. After the main meal, there would be a variety of Myanmar sweetmeats like *sanwinmakin, thagu,* or *kyaukyaw;* fruits of the season; and always some bananas to fill up any empty spaces left in the stomach. Pickled tea leaf, called *laphet,* with its accompaniment of fried garlic, beans, nuts, and sesame seeds, was a never-absent item on the menu. It rounded off the meal. A cup of thick, creamy coffee was an omnipresent staple, too. Pho Pho had a standing invitation for my family. We children knew that special food was in the offing if we visited the zayat on those *Upoke* days.

On days of special religious significance, like the full-moon days, Pho Pho would insist that the families of his children come to join him at the zayat to take the Eight Precepts from the presiding monk at the Bagaya Tawya Monastery. On these occasions, our families would bring special offerings for the monks, such as robes, or edible supplies for the monastery. We would also bring one or two special dishes as our contribution to the meal offered to the monks. Before the offering of *Soon* is the special service for the granting of the Eight Precepts. We would sit facing the *Sayardaw,* with Pho Pho at the centre in the front row with the elder aunts and uncles, and the rest of us behind them. We would intone, after the monk, the sacred vows to keep the Eight Precepts. The elders and the older children knew the words by heart, but the youngest child among us grandchildren, perhaps a year or two old, felt perfectly happy to join the general incantation by mumbling whatever sounded right to him. This assembly was Pho Pho's way of ensuring that we made merit together so that we would meet again in our subsequent lives before we achieved nibbana.

In contrast, in the lives we lead in these modern times, we could not afford to stay home for those Upoke days and we miss out on embracing religious contemplation and meditation. Even on the big holidays, like the Kason (full moon), some modern-day Buddhists may allow social commitments to encroach or may decide to spend the time on some urgent things that had been waiting to be addressed during the rest of the week. All too often, these holidays become like any other day off, spent by resting or having fun. A day when we observe the sanctity of the occasion with a *soon kyway* (a morning meal for invited monks), when *parittas* once were recited and prayers said, has become a rarity.

It has to be said that this trend is not purely the result of a lack of inclination. Everyday lives in this modern age have become so complicated and so hassled that any extra arrangements needing to be made, as for a *soon kyway,* can only be attended to after much planning and deliberation. Gone are the days when we could rely on a whole fleet of household help, be they live-in relatives or paid servants, to prepare the variety of food usually offered at a meal for the monks, and to serve them in the special customary way. On holidays in the past, the variety of food would entail, at the bare minimum, chicken and two or three other kinds of meat, fish, prawns, and a choice array of vegetables, either stir-fried or as salads. The sweetmeats course would often be of an overwhelming variety. In today's times, the nuclear family, often with both husband and wife working, has replaced the big, rambling family consisting of two or three generations, where spinster sisters or aunts helped look after the children and did the housekeeping. Relatives too, even those that were not living with the family, would, in those days, have time to volunteer their services at a big or small *ahlu*. Everyone loved these occasions because they were a chance to catch up on the gossip, enjoy jokes together, and eat together at big, round tables, all at the expense of the *ahlushin*.

Since the monks are not allowed to ask for extra helpings or reach across the table, the hosts have to see that everything the monks might need is handed to them. It is important to keep a watchful eye on the monks so one can fill up their plates with rice or replenish their soup bowls. Most times, the monks do not even cast their eyes over the whole table and are not even be aware of what all has been offered. They take just what they see in the line of vision of their downcast eyes. Thus, it is the duty of the hosts to see that each item is offered for the monks to accept or cast aside.

Nevertheless, enough occasions arise in the course of a year for a Buddhist family to choose to make one of these into a special event by inviting the monks for a meal to break their fast at the hour of dawn or for the main meal before noon. Such occasions include birthdays and wedding anniversaries of family members, commemorative events for the birthdays, or the memorial days of departed ones. Also celebrated in such a way are the special religious days of the full moon of significant months: Kason, Waso, Thadingyut, and Tazaunmon.

Kason falls in the month of May, which is the peak of the Myanmar dry season. From time immemorial, the full-moon day of Kason has been celebrated with the offering of water at the base of the sacred bo tree, sacred because it was at the base of a bo tree that Buddha attained Enlightenment. In villages and in Myanmar quarters of Yangon, special religious associations would organize a procession of young maidens, each carrying a clay pot of water on her head or hitching it on her hip, to make their way to the nearest pagoda within whose precincts there would be a bo tree. This procession would be accompanied on foot by a music ensemble consisting of an oboe, a wooden clapper, and drums called the *dobat* played with a staccato beat. This ensemble is characteristically called the *dobat-waing.* The *Shwe Yo* dance, which is choreographed in a comic and rustic fashion, usually is the centre of attraction. Thus villages and Myanmar quarters would resound with the music of these dobat-waing either in the early morning or early afternoon of the Kason full-moon day.

The full moon of Waso has special religious significance, as this is the day on which Buddha preached the first sermon to the five ascetics. It also marked the beginning of the Buddhist Lent. The offering of Waso robes to the sangha is a special ceremony that many families and institutions observe on the full-moon day of Waso and the days that follow. Waso is also noted for the special day after the full moon when young people form into groups to gather wild flowers in the most likely wooded areas. By this time of the year, the first rains have fallen and the whole countryside is lush and green. A variety of wild flowers grow. Special among these is the *padein-ngo,* a flower with delicate tendrils and so finely wrought, as if in a golden filigree, that it would bring the finest craftsman to tears in despair of achieving its exquisite likeness, for thus is the meaning of its name. It is the Waso flower par excellence. These flowers, gathered by the young people with much gaiety and merriment, with song and laughter, are then offered at the various pagodas in the vicinity. This tradition is called the Gathering of Waso Flowers. It was generally celebrated in our young days with student associations from both universities and other schools making special excursions to woodlands on these occasions.

Thadingyut heralds the end of Buddhist Lent and the end of the rainy season. The bright skies make possible outdoor festivities like the *zat* and the *pwe,* which are beloved by the Myanmar people. *Anyeint pwes* are held to entertain guests at weddings and during special occasions like the *shinpyu.* In fact, it epitomizes the grandeur of any occasion to stage an anyeint pwe. It is the ultimate honour to have one laid out for your birthday or wedding or some anniversary. Since it is in the open air, not only invited guests but also people in the neighbourhood can all crowd around to enjoy the dances and songs of the *minthar* and *minthamee,* and the ribaldry of the clowns. The joyous music of the *saing waing* and the drums reverberate around the neighbourhood, very much a sign of the time of year. Night bazaars would sometimes spring up in the vicinity of these pwes, lit by flaring torches. And people from far and near would come to walk along the lanes made narrow by the encroaching stalls selling the biggest variety of Myanmar food and snacks, among them foods that are available only at that time of year, such as sticky rice cooked in bamboo stems, and roasted crickets. People of our generation caught only the tail end of this era of pwes, but even so I can still remember the magic of attending a performance such as this. There was the special excitement of going out at night, a rare opportunity for us at that time, dressing up for it, and beholding a brightly lit festival aura in the open air. The beautiful dancers on stage, in glittering dresses and dancing with such gaiety and abandon, the throbbing music, and the whole magical ambience was such as to leave one with an indelible memory of the occasion.

Thadingyut is special to the lives of the Myanmar people for many reasons. For the farmers, it is the season of harvest, when crops are sold and the farmers' grinding hard work has paid off, putting ready cash in their pockets. For the young men and women all over the country, it is an eagerly awaited time, because the customary ban on marriage during the months of Lent is lifted. For everyone who likes fun and gaiety, this is the season when the oppressive rain slowly fades away with the retreat of the monsoon winds, and games and entertainment are possible in the open air. Buddhist families who like to uphold the religious tradition of paying respects to their elders celebrate Lent as a special occasion when young and old in the family reaffirm their relationships. In my time, my parents would take us children to Kyimyindine, where most of our maternal grandaunts and granduncles lived. Kyimyindine and all predominantly Myanmar quarters like Ahlone have pwes and night markets, so the residences are all lit up with lanterns or candles or little earthen containers of oil and lighted wicks. We children would be delighted to show off our new clothes, have an outing in the festive atmosphere, be treated to sweet confections, and made much of by the grandaunt or granduncle to whom we had come to pay respects with our own offering of sweetmeats or fruit. Most often we were specially delighted and gleeful to have handed to us, each in turn, a gift of usually a small amount of pocket money by our elders.

Pho Pho, who passed away at the age of eighty in 1953, was attended most devotedly in his last days by his spinster daughter Ngwe and his two youngest sons, all of whom lived with him. With his passing, the centre of gravity dissolved. Because there was no longer a pulling force, the children rarely met regularly as a big extended family.

My brothers and I, once we became parents in our turn, kept alive most vigilantly this Thadingyut tradition for our children while they were young. Very early on, perhaps a month ahead of Thadingyut, my sisters-in-law and I would confer to determine which items we would like to offer to our aunts and uncles. Sometimes we would buy oranges or sweet limes by the hundreds at the wholesale fruit market. With perhaps ten or twelve of these fruits as the base gift, we would add our own individual offering depending on the circumstances of the elders. Would our relatives better appreciate an article of clothing, such as a *pasoe* or a *longyi,* or would they prefer dry provisions like a tin of Milo or coffee or biscuits? We could be very creative both in the variety and in the arrangement of the *kadaw pyitsi,* trying to make the gift basket or the tray look its most attractive.

In the 1980s, only my brother Htut and his wife, Pyone, could afford a car, a red Sunny pickup. With a generosity of spirit, which somehow we all expected of, and found in, each other, Htut and Pyone were always willing to take the rest of us to the places we wanted to go. Instead of feeling deprived and sorry, the rest of us were happy that one of us had the means to own a vehicle. Like the Three Musketeers, we were all for one and one for all. So our seven children, and the adults, whoever happened to be in town, would happily squash ourselves inside the pickup and visit the houses of our aunts and uncles and older cousins. It was even more fun as we shared stories and jokes on the way. Having paid our respects to our aunts and uncles, we would all come back to our parents' house. All of us sat on mats before the two of them, who beamed at this assembly from their chairs. I have to admit that we four siblings did vie with each other to make this Thadingyut offering to our parents more special than the others in one way or another. Here again, Pyone and Htut had an advantage, because Pyone was receiving a continuous supply of hard-to-get provisions from her parents, who lived in Bangkok. For that was the socialist era, our dark days, and we Myanmar people made do with the most basic items like cooking oil sold to us from the People's Stores on a strict quota, controlled by a household member's list. Chocolates and apples and Coca-Cola were very rare indulgences indeed. After we adults paid our obeisance to our parents, the hungry kids fell upon the delicious spread concocted by their grandmother with the help of her trusted and skilful cook, Ma Pyone Kyi. At about that time, my son Aung Thura, the oldest grandchild, was thirteen, and Tun Htut, who was Pyone and Htut's second son, was three and the youngest grandchild.

Thingyan, which brings in our New Year, is perhaps the most rousingly boisterous celebration of all our festivals. Yet it has to be remembered that there are many facets to its celebration and there are many ways in which this festival is celebrated by people of different ages. It takes place in the hottest month of the year. The water that is doused, sprayed, or splattered on with *Eugenia caryophyllus* leaves is meant to cleanse away the sins and the impurities of the old year. So people are not supposed to get angry when water is thrown at them, as their sins and bad effects are being washed away. As young children, we were provided with metal bowls (before plastic became prevalent), or tin water guns and a bucket or drum full of water, to use for spraying water on any passer-by who accepted it either under protest or in convivial spirit. Laughing adults would sometimes turn round and grab the bucket from us to return the favour.

In Pho Pho's time, his children and grandchildren were most often at the zayat every day of the four or five days when Thingyan was celebrated. The children would be running around and throwing water at each other or on passers-by, or watching the revellers as they roamed the city in decorated cars. Our aunts would be in the kitchen cooking the midday meal and the special festive food that they had decided to make for that day. This could be any of a great variety of Thingyan foods, such as *shwe yin aye* or *mont lon yay baw* or vermicelli soup. These were always made in ample amounts so that jugs and bowlfuls of these drinks and soups could be sent around to neighbouring zayats so that the whole household could eat to their hearts' content all day. In the same way, our neighbours would send us their special food for the day. In this way, we all had many things to eat. Many of the elders kept the Eight Precepts. Two or three round tables had to be laid for them to partake of a scrumptious meal well in time before noon.

Instead of seeing Thingyan as merely a time for revelry, many people welcomed the New Year with different ways of gaining merit, something which is important for our Buddhist people on this auspicious occasion. In certain quarters of the city, young people do service to

Ko Ko Tommy, Ma Ma Lily, Ma Ma Sweety, and me at the zayat, 1950s

their elders by washing their hair with *tayaw* and *kimpun*, preparing *thanakha* paste for their use, or even cutting their nails for them, things which normally an elderly person would find difficult to do on his or her own. Some young people organize groups to set free fish into lakes and ponds. There are those who spend the entire holidays in a meditation retreat or at a monastery. Many individuals and groups set up temporary structures where people are offered special Thingyan food. Called *satudithar,* these are events where food is given free to any and all comers.

As we grew into our teens, we graduated from playing by the roadside to joining other young people at a *mandat* hastily or elaborately erected for the occasion, from which to douse people with water from hose pipes connected to a nearby water source.

Mandalay, as the cultural capital of the country, always celebrates Thingyan in grand style. Mandalay organized big decorative floats. One of these was spectacular in the shape of a big white swan, complete with music and dance troupes ensconced on it. The organizers had spent the previous two or three months composing and rehearsing songs and dances. These decorated floats representing a region or an association went around to the specially designated pandals, where prizes were awarded for best decoration or best music or best dance. This parade of decorated floats happened only at night, after the water play, while invited guests were seated in armchairs. Other spectators stood crowded around, clapping and singing along with the performers on the floats. During the day, these venues would have their own programmes of song and dance whilst a bevy of girls manned an alarming battery of hose pipes to douse the Thingyan revellers who had arrived on a big assortment of transport: open jeeps, trucks, motorbikes, and bicycles – or on foot.

Thingyan being celebrated joyfully in front of the city hall and in view of the Sule Pagoda in Yangon city centre, 2015

Chapter 6

Summer in the Hills

Every summer from the time our father was assistant traffic manager of the Burma Railways, he would take us children on a trip to the hill station of Kalaw in his inspection coach. Although this inspection coach became bigger and relatively grander as he rose higher in position, each one had the same features, which made travelling by train very convenient and so much like being home away from home, with all the added excitement. There was the kitchen section, in the charge of a train attendant who also did the cooking for us; a small bathroom with toilet combined; a sleeping section with two beds and two upper bunks; and a reception area. The reception area was where father received the district officials of the Burma Railways as we reached each stop on the way, when they would discuss official business.

As many times as we went on these trips, they never failed to delight us. The preparation for such a trip concerned us only when it came to deciding what clothes to take and what items to bring for our entertainment. But for Mother, she packed a wooden trunk called a "line trunk" (because it was to be used when going on a trip on the railway line, or so I assumed). This she packed with supplies of rice, oil, potatoes, onions, and coffee, and tinned goods and similar dry provisions. She would also prepare roasted and fried dried fish, and *balachaung* and pickled mangoes and similar condiments, to supplement the food that the attendant would cook for us on the way. The coach had, attached at the back, a little cage-like contraption where chicken were kept (for obvious reasons). But we rarely used that, since both my parents were conscientious Buddhists and the thought of bringing some live animal which was pretty soon to be dispatched with and brought to the table to satisfy our appetites was against their teachings. However, we children used that little cage once and with disastrous results. It taught us a valuable lesson, which is never to treat a life carelessly and thoughtlessly. We were given an owl that was caught by one of the staff members who manned the rest house in Kalaw. Unthinkingly, and in ignorance, we decided to bring the bird home in the little cage at the back of the carriage. On arriving at a station on the way, we went to see how it was faring and found it quite dead and stiff on its perch. Our father explained to us that owls could not withstand the daylight, then he reminded us that we should not do anything unthinkingly and without consulting our parents. We children were desolate at the thought that the poor bird had suffered because of our thoughtless action.

The four of us were always good company among ourselves, although what we liked best was to gaze out of the windows of the carriage from the comfort of the bed or from a chair in the front section. With our arms resting on the window ledge and our chins on our forearms, with the wind riffling through our hair, we would let our imaginations run wild. Occasionally we would witness some funny or unusual sight, and then we would call out to each other to come and see two buffaloes with horns locked, ramming against each other, or a small foal following her mother around, or a flock of ducks swimming in a small pond by the side of the railway. We would be moved by the enchantment of seeing a small, lonely hut in a vast field with smoke curling up from its hearth. Suddenly shook out of our reverie by some pangs of hunger, we would get up to see what was laid on the small dining table. Perhaps there was some sticky rice and fried chicken, perhaps some fried sparrows, or perhaps some steamed sticky rice with a banana filling – all of these foods bought from the hawkers that crowd around the open windows of the carriages when a stop is made in the towns along the line. I only remember that there was a great variety of snacks and we were hungry very often. The rolling gait of the carriage as it clattered along the tracks seemed to help our digestive processes. Father and Mother would also be gazing out at the scenery, from the comfort of their chairs, also lost in thought, because conversation was a little difficult as the train rattled along its tracks. Glancing back at them, we would catch them looking at us fondly. We would then exchange contented smiles as if to say, "We are all here together, and that is all that matters."

Once or twice, the boys engaged in antics that could have ended in disaster. Htut, who was in his "Cowboys and Indians" phase, tried to lasso the small trees that grew along the railway tracks. He was lucky that neither his rope-knotting skills nor his lassoing techniques were what they should have been. In Kalaw, Moe fell into a small stream that lay in a little gully in front of the railway siding where our coach was parked. Although the stream was small and quite shallow, the little boy was smaller still. Mishap was avoided only because his elder brother had quickly pulled him out.

Father always made us bring notebooks where we went so we could write down the names of the stations as we passed them and to record bits of information like how far up the area was from sea level and what produce we saw being loaded at the stops. But the beauty of the scenery, and the interesting images along the line, whetted my imagination and prompted me to write descriptive passages as well, which later appeared as a short article in my school magazine.

Very often, we had our friends or relatives join us on these trips. It got a little crowded then, but we didn't mind. The more the merrier was how we saw it. As far as sleeping space was concerned, we just had to be a little adaptable. My parents always had the main beds, we children shared the bunk beds, and the elders among our guests used the two collapsible beds in the front section. If there were more people, then the whole of the living area was cleared of chairs and tables, and sleeping gear was laid on the floor of the carriage. Then we would sleep on the makeshift mattresses, all in a row. It was summer and it was never cold on the way; we might have felt the cold only when we were in the hills. Once in Kalaw, we either stayed on in the carriage, which had been shunted onto the siding, or we went up to stay at the Kalaw rest house, which was fully furnished. There were tennis courts close to where our carriages were parked. Although there were mostly adults from the Kalaw Railways office playing there, we older children could sometimes go and play there.

Our days in Kalaw were always full of activities. As often as not, there would be other coaches belonging to our father's colleagues, who were there with their families. Sometimes we would team up with them to take sightseeing trips, in jeeps provided by the local officials, to interesting places like the Kalaw reservoir. We enjoyed picnics under the pine trees, or we went visiting friends from Yangon who had a summer house there and who would entertain us with a splendid lunch. Fresh and exotic leafy vegetables were served as dips with a relish made of salted soya beans. There were delicious soups made from these vegetables picked fresh from the hillside gardens that very morning and, perhaps also, venison that had become available at the five-day market. And to top it all off there were fresh strawberries, which we children liked best mashed and mixed with a lot of condensed milk, gooey-sweet and lip-smacking good. In fact, our favourite picnic fare in Kalaw, as we sat on fallen pine needles on a gentle slope of the hill at the back of the railway station, was strawberries picked from the fields and condensed milk straight from the tins, the latter of which we had bought that morning.

My mother at Kalaw with her favourite purchase: orchid plants

One fond memory I have of my mother, for whom grocery shopping was a passion, was how she would quite go overboard when indulging in the Kalaw

37

markets. She would come back with two or three big baskets topped with leafy greens and huge heads of cauliflower, her arms laden with flowering orchid plants. Indigenous orchids were found in plenty in the Shan states. Her favourites were the blue vandas and the small, waxy yellow variety which are called candle flowers.

Sometimes, instead of going to Kalaw, we went to the hill station of Maymyo for a change. But there was then no railway line to that town. So we got off at Mandalay and took the nearly two or three hours' winding drive up to Maymyo. Nowadays this same trip is billed as a one to two-hour drive. There were more interesting places to visit around Maymyo even then, such as the Pwe Kauk Falls and the Peikchinmyaung Caves. In the town itself, the botanical garden was an attraction, and the drive to it in a horse-drawn carriage was a special treat for us. But we rarely stayed more than a day or two, preferring to make our base in Kalaw.

In a way, the two towns were interchangeable as small, sleepy hill resorts where one went to escape the heat of the plains in the summer and enjoy the quiet life of the countryside. The scene of cosy little bungalows nestled in the hillsides with small gardens ablaze with flowers created the same effect. But Kalaw boasted of more hilly pine woods, good for climbs and picnicking. The sound of the wind whistling through the pines and the lonely cry of the greater coucal, or *bokekaung,* were sleep-inducing. One time, a friend of mine and I were nearly left behind because we had fallen asleep in one of the bedrooms of the otherwise empty and echoing old rest house.

In time, though, Maymyo, now known as Pyin Oo Lwin, came to be more developed, having become the preferred site for holiday homes for the military brass, and the well-to-do from Mandalay and Yangon. As the home of the military institutes like the Defence Services Academy (DSA), the Defence Services Medical Academy (DSMA), and the Defence Services Technological Academy (DSTA), Maymyo sees the influx of the parents and the guests of students of these academies, in addition to the chiefs of staff of the army, navy, and air force – and their entourages – each year at graduation. The botanical gardens have also been upgraded to a much larger complex, now known as the Kandawgyi National Park, a 437-acre park with a 70-acre lake, forestland, a viewing tower, a medicinal plant garden, and rose, bamboo, and orchid gardens. Black swans imported from Australia grace the beautiful lake at its centre. The small pagoda stands as before, at one edge of the lake, and cherry blossoms in season are reflected in its placid waters.

Back then, Maymyo became for us more than a holiday venue when, in 1963, Moe attended a summer camp of the University Training Corps (UTC), of which he had become a volunteer member when he entered the University of Rangoon. The UTC were being trained in handling small arms and munitions and as squad leaders of a platoon of eleven infantrymen. Moe came to visit us at the railway siding on his free pass days. Then Polay (Linn Myaing) joined the Defence Services Academy in 1964 for the eleventh intake of the military college, which awards a BSc after four years. In 1968, our father and mother attended Polay's graduation and saw him receive the prize of a gold medal for academic excellence.

Although Kalaw was the favourite place for us as our vacation destination, we often went along to other places on the railway line as Father went about his official business. Thus we would find ourselves parked on a lonely siding in such places as Myitnge or Kyaukpadaung. It would be quite hot in the coach, and the water supply limited, so when the stationmaster and his wife came to invite us to their home to relax and take a satisfying bath, we would accept happily and take the chance to sluice ourselves with bucketfuls of water. Neither could Mother and I refuse the offer of the use of the stationmaster's wife's *kyaukpyin* and *thanakha*. We put generous applications of these on our faces and limbs. The cooling and fragrant effect of the thanakha was immediate and exquisite. Then the adults would exchange pleasantries over an enticing dish of laphet and cups of Shan tea, after which we would thank our gracious hosts and return to the carriage.

Moe attends the UTC summer
camp and visits his family at the
Kalaw Railway Station

DSA graduation in 1968; Linn
Myaing awarded the gold medal
for academic excellence

Chapter 7

Five-Day Markets

The five-day markets are a special feature which visitors as well as the local people enjoy in the Shan states. Neighbouring towns each have their own five-day markets. The days are staggered so that the produce sellers can go to each of the surrounding towns in turn to sell their wares. Thus towns in the hill stations of Kalaw and Aungpan will have their markets on different days of the week. And the bigger circuit is Taunggyi, Nyaungshwe, Shwenyaung, Heho, and Pindaya, where the markets are bigger and attract bigger crowds and more business.

These markets take on the characteristics of a county fair. But they are even more colourful since ethnic variety is a huge element. In my day, all the hill tribes, such as the Pa Oh, Palaungs, and Danu, in their distinctive tribal costumes and headgear, with silver ornaments around their necks or arms and legs, would congregate on the town. Their wares of cherry-red tomatoes, glistening green peppers, and snowy-white heads of cauliflower would be bundled into huge baskets that they carried straddled on their foreheads. They had made their way from the villages high up on the mountainsides, starting their journey in the dim darkness of early morning and then travelling through a landscape misty with the vapours of the mountains. At the market, they would spread their fresh-picked leafy vegetables, root vegetables, and onions and garlic on mats or pieces of cloth, using a weighing scale of quite distinctive design. Flowers were banked in colourful profusion in big bamboo baskets. There would be a babble of tongues, and everywhere would be movement and colour in a huge kaleidoscope. Strange and exotic plants, and sometimes even animal hides and antlers, would be on sale. Chillies in huge mounds were spread on mats, and strings of white bulbs of garlic made colourful displays.

There were stalls selling food special to the region, mostly Shan in origin, like tofu salad and noodles with pickled mustard and yellow rice balls. We made a point of savouring these regional foods, for we felt that here we would get an authentic version. One sure mark of the authenticity of the foods was the red-hot chillies and the liberal use of garlic. Both chillies and garlic were served as accompaniments. Men and women in turbans sat around drinking Shan tea and enjoying the food after an arduous morning of commerce. Then there were delicious Nepalese or Indian sweets made from thick, creamy milk obtained from herds bred on the verdant mountainside.

We also frequented the shops in the more permanent section of the market, which had cement floors and was roofed with corrugated iron. This section had stalls sectioned off. These stalls sold anything from a great variety of cheap household goods and farm implements, to bolts of textiles, to woollen clothes and silverware. The silver here is mixed with a metal known locally as *baw,* from the nearby mines of Namtu. We were fascinated with the array of attractive silver jewellery, the bangles and bracelets and rings and buttons. The boys had their own shopping to do, and that was for miniature Shan daggers, which were meant to be more ornamental than functional. Every year the boys would bring back one or two daggers, and every year we girls would buy silver jewellery as gifts for one or the other of our friends.

One whole morning was never enough on these market days as we dawdled over the vast array of unbelievably fresh fruits and vegetables. We would end up buying more of everything than we needed. And although we haggled over the price for the fun of it, we would always give in at the first refusal. With so much to see, the foods we wanted to sample, and the time taken to choose presents for our friends back home, it was always way past our usual lunchtime before we could leave the market. It was a good thing our mother had sent ahead the maid or the train attendant with a basketful of groceries with which to prepare our lunch. By the time we got back, hot, tired, and hungry – and in a horse-drawn carriage – the collapsible dining table would already be laid with a variety of dishes. The fresh vegetables, especially the leafy greens, were given top billing in soups, salads, and dips.

Since it was the time-honoured custom to bring back gifts from whatever travels we undertook, Mother would also be buying basket-loads of Shan garlic or packets of tea and orchid plants to give away once we got back to Yangon. Our railway carriage kitchen area was always stuffed full of these regional products. What's more, Mother would be buying more items as we rode back the railway line: shiny, thin-skinned onions from Thazi, roasted duck from Nyaunglebin, barbecued fish on skewers, and so on. Two times, we children were able to persuade our parents to let us bring back an adorable Shan puppy. Polay, who had grown up with a family dog, a dog that was always within his playful reach since he was barely a toddler, is the sibling who is crazy about dogs. Although all four of us would make a big fuss about the puppy, it was he who took care of it in the long run. But sadly we came to realize that the heat of the plains in Yangon was not the ideal climate for a furry Shan dog, so we desisted from bringing back others in later years.

One feature of the five-day market which lay outside the sphere of things we were allowed to do but which fascinated us nevertheless was that some of the stalls were set up with four-animal gambling roulette. The roulette game board was just a simple rough piece of square cloth with pictures of the four animals – a pig, a hen, a snake, and a frog – laid on the dirt floor. Bets would be placed on the square of the chosen animal and the dice would be rolled. Four or five men in towel turbans would be hunkering around and making bets; there would be a few others standing around and watching. This was a favourite game at the annual gambling pwes, which used to be held in the Shan states for centuries. The Bawgyo Pwe, held on the premises of the Bawgyo Pagoda in Hsipaw, was the most famous of these. Inge Sargent, for ten years the mahadevi of Hsibaw as consort of the then ruling Shan prince, described this Bagywo Pwe in detail in her book *Twilight over Burma.*

It was well known that the locals were very fond of this type of gambling. The entire livelihood of hard-working farmers could be lost in a day at the gambling tables. In order to prevent such damaging consequences for these simple folk, the Shan *sawbwas* in their time, and later the union government, took steps to limit the number of pwes held each year and subsequently banned all types of gambling at these markets.

Chapter 8

Favourite Cousins

Being the only girl in the family, I yearned for like company now and then. My favourite cousins at the time were the daughters of Mother's elder half-sister, our Kyee Kyee Lay. Theirs was a family of three boys and two girls. The eldest brother and the sisters were all older than I. I loved going to spend time with them during school holidays and weekends. Sometimes both Htut and I would go to spend a couple of days or even a whole week with them as a special treat. Htut had his playmate in George, and I had my yearned-for company in *Ma Ma* Lily and Ma Ma Sweety. In the daytime I would help them with little chores around the house or help Kyee Kyee Lay in the kitchen. Just doing things together was a lot of fun, especially with older cousins.

Kyee Kyee Lay was a very gentle and religious person. She took every opportunity to teach us children the values that are important for Buddhists. She would tell us why *dhana,* or the act of giving, is important, and go on to tell us the story of King Vesandara in the Jataka tales whose acts of dhana could never be outdone. She would point out to us why patience and forbearance should be cultivated. She told us the story of Saddhan, the Elephant King, as an example of the ultimate act of forbearance. And so on and so forth.

And we children, from a very young age, were made familiar with these stories as told by elders, dramatized as zat pwes, and lyricized as songs heard on every festive religious day. Kyee Kyee Lay would even trick us into doing merit by telling us children that a watermelon drink would be sweeter if we recited the *Thambode'* mantra while stirring sugar into it. On long, hot summer days when we children were hot and thirsty, the thought of making a watermelon drink as sweet as possible was a powerful incentive.

In the evenings after dinner, we girls would lie on the bed and talk about clothes. On thinking back, I don't see what there was to say about our clothes, which consisted of a regular top and a never-varying wrap-around longyi. True, we could choose colours and prints, but the style then was invariably the same for every female, young or old. Oh yes, we could choose the material, silk or cotton or satin, but cotton is for every day, and silk or satin is for special occasions. And that was as far as it went. But strangely enough, we had lots to talk about when it came to our clothes: which occasion merited what type of clothes, the accessories (i.e. hair clips and ribbons) that should go with the outfit, whether we should all dress alike, thereby engaging in our favourite practice of *sin tu,* and whether we should have different colours of the same design (and who would choose which colour this time). We debated the pros and the cons in a never-ending rigmarole. We loved it; we relished it. And we would dramatize the start of each session with one of us announcing in suitably weighty tones, "*Asi Asin*" (meaning "programme" or "agenda"). The occasions for which we would be choosing clothes were birthday parties, which were rather rare in those days; *soon kyways,* which took place more often; or family gatherings for the festive occasions like Thadingyut and Tazaungdine. The one occasion which stood out and which I still remember is, of course, the Independence Day celebrations at the Burma Railways office, to which my father invited my cousins. I, Ma Ma Sweety, and Ma Ma Lily decided to dress alike in pink silk longyis in a geometric pattern. The variation was in the way we styled our hair and the hair accessories we used. I was just ten, so wearing a longyi was a special, grown-up treat.

My cousins lived in a small bungalow on a small rise on University Avenue. The bungalow was small, but it was built towards the back of a huge compound. The mango tree, which still survives today, was young and vigorous in those days and bore a huge amount of delicious fruits every year. The trunk was thick and the branches spreading; it was ideal for us children to play under during the heat of the day. By March or April, there would be green, young fruit, which we children loved to eat with salt because the mangoes were so sour. It made us salivate just to think of it. We would take with us a packet of salt wrapped in a scrap of newspaper, encamp under the tree, and, after dipping the fruits in salt, eat the ones that had fallen off the tree. The elders discouraged us from picking the young mangoes, but it was very easy for one of the boys to climb high enough on one of the stout branches to beat down a bunch or two. One day when the fruits were nearly ripened, there was a big storm, as sometimes accompanied the onset of the monsoons, and almost all the mangoes were shaken loose from the tree. While the wind raged and rain pounded on the roof, we stayed huddled in the house, feeling awed and excited by the ferocity of the elements, at the same time enjoying the safety of being inside the house among family. Once the wind calmed down and the rain slowed to a drizzle, we couldn't contain ourselves anymore and went outside to pick the mangoes that lay thick on the ground. The boys next door, the Aung Chein brothers, came over to help us pick the fruits and carry them inside the house in big baskets. It was the first time I met Tun Aung and Than Aung. My brother and I later became great friends with them, our friendships lasting well into our senior years. We were barely into our teens at the time of our first meeting.

In 1951, our cousin Tin Tun, the eldest of Kyee Kyee Lay's children (later to become Lieutenant General Tin Tun, air chief and deputy prime minister during the State Law and Order Restoration Council (SLORC) era) and two others from the burgeoning Burma Air Force (BAF) were sent as cadets for training in Cranwell after completing solo flight training in Mingaladon. At the same time, a small group of navy cadets including Maung Maung Khin (later Lieutenant General Maung Maung Khin, navy chief of staff and deputy prime minister, also during SLORC era) went to Dartmouth and another group of army cadets including Maung Maung were sent to Sandhurst. They were the first group of Burmese military cadets to be sent to do their training in the United Kingdom under a programme sponsored by the UK government. Tin Tun was a champion pole-vaulter at university, being an imposing 5'11" and bearing a striking resemblance, with his dark, wavy hair and strong features, to the then hugely popular Peter Lawford, the Hollywood star. He spent three years at Cranwell, after which he earned his wings and returned to the BAF as a fighter pilot. He became a Top Gun.

In 1954, Tin Tun was again chosen to attend a Pilot Attack Trainer course, this time a shorter one and taking place in several venues like Hull and Wales. There he became friends with Michael Armitage, who was later knighted. In 1987 when Tin Tun went to London to have an eye operation, he was put up at the Wimbledon home of the Burmese military attaché in London. Sir Michael invited General Tin Tun to tea at the RAF Club near Buckingham Palace. He had his namesake, the Burmese ambassador, for company on the occasion.

Six years and nine years my junior, respectively, my two younger brothers had their constant playmates in Zut, Gut, and Lut, the three younger sons of our uncle U Htwe Maung. My uncle Htwe was a chief scout in Burma and had attended jamborees in Thailand, Indonesia, and the USA. He encouraged his sons and nephews who were of age to join the movement. Whenever the cousins were together, they would play from morning till dark, only coming in to gulp down their food at mealtimes and after hearing repeated pleas that they throw bucketfuls of water on themselves to have a rudimentary bath. I remember that they got themselves into incredible scrapes. Once they had a brainwave to catch a vulture by pretending to be corpses. This was in the Municipal Corporation–owned house on Mt. Pleasant occupied by our uncle Htwe, who was chief accountant for the said corporation. Incredibly, my children and their cousins, at the playful age came up with a similar idea. They wanted to catch the kites which they saw wheeling high above in the blue skies of our cold season. They wheedled chicken legs and necks from our cook, tied them to a string, and placed them one piece at a time on a little clearing. Then they waited in ambush. Whatever the flaws of this strategy, it never worked. But at least this prank had no risk of danger.

Once, the cousins dared each other to crash their fists through a glass pane. There was always a mastermind among them who thought up these wild schemes and succeeded in egging on a more gullible member. It was Moe who took up the dare, smashing his fist right through the little square pane of glass. His hand came out gashed at the knuckles. The searing pain of the glass cutting his hand didn't have time to register before the sight of the blood oozing out made him faint clean away.

And there were the times the cousins played at soldiers and captains. Once the captain ordered his men to dig a hole in the ground. When the boys figured it would be easier to dig wet ground, the captain came up with a brilliant idea to have his men make this happen in the easiest, quickest way they knew how.

Sweety, Win, Lily, and me at 73 University Avenue,
house of my cousins

Chapter 9

St Philomena's Convent

St Philomena's Convent, situated on Pyay Road, was one out of several missionary schools that were operating in Yangon, Mandalay, Mawlamyine, and other big towns in Myanmar until the early 1960s. Missionary schools had been in Myanmar, as in the Indian subcontinent, since the eighteenth century, when they followed close behind the colonial expansion into the region. It is well known that ideological imperialists believed that their mission was to "civilize" the local population. They saw missionaries as the "predestined agents" of the civilizing empire. In 1856, the most well-known personage of the Catholic missionaries to Burma, Monsignor Bigandet, was appointed vicar for Ava and Pegu, i.e. for divided Myanmar, by the Society for Foreign Missions of Paris (Missions Etrangères de Paris (MEP)). Bigandet studied the Burmese language and succeeded in composing his *Prayer Book in Burmese* within two years of his first arrival in Mergui. As a scholar, he took an interest in the religion of the host country and visited monasteries, read Pali commentaries, and discussed religion with the monks and even with King Mindon, who had received him very graciously. *The Life or Legend of Gaudama* was published in 1858 as a fruit of this study.

In the early twentieth century, schools were conducted by the Brothers of the Christian Schools and by the Sisters of the Good Shepherd, of St Joseph of the Apparition, and of St Francis Xavier.

In Rangoon, St Philomena's Convent on Pyay Road, St John's Convent, St Francis Convent, and the diocesan high school were schools run by Catholic nuns for girls. Boys were admitted only up till the fourth standard. All of these schools had boarding facilities. The Irish Catholic nuns were very strict with the girls. In fact, they were very quick to punish the Anglo-Indian and Anglo-Burmese girls who made up more than a quarter of the students in a class. One Mother Anne, for example, did not hesitate to slap a student and make her kneel in front of the class. We were agape and horrified when this happened. I don't think our parents would have accepted such humiliating treatment if it were meted out to us. We were terrified of the nuns, who would often brandish a cane in class. However, it was not all of them who were severe in their dealings with students. There were some who were almost beatific in their demeanour, and as kindly in their actions.

There was another trademark peculiar to these convents, and that was their insistence that Myanmar students take on Western names so that it would be easier for the nuns to pronounce and remember the names. That had been the case since our parents' time, and it had continued on to ours. Whoever went to a missionary school instead of a national school most likely ended up with an Anglo name in addition to his or her Myanmar name. The latter was the name which had been given a child at birth. It was based on astrological readings at the time and on the day of the child's birth, and it was subsequently inscribed in the child's palm-leaf horoscopes, or *zartars.* So, when faced with the prospect of having to produce an Anglo name, we would – although it was not our custom to specify a family or surname – assume our father's name as the surname. The peculiarity of this, of course, was that our fathers' names may have had no element of their own parents' name in them, so the names were in no way family names as is understood in some cultures.

Some Myanmar parents made a point of refusing this practice for their children. A friend of mine and a string of her sisters were each registered under new names when they entered St John's Convent. When they came home and their father was apprised of this, he was indignant. He went to the Mother Superior the next morning and insisted that his daughters be registered in their original names or else he would not leave them in that school. He won his point. It has to be conceded, though, that the father's name had to be included in the children's names just so that they could be identified as coming from the same family. It would have been too confusing for the nuns to remember, for example, that Hla Kyi and Mya Khin and Hnin Si, with completely diverse names, were sisters without the addition of their father's name at the end!

School concerts were a regular feature at these convents. They consisted of fundraising events or sometimes just a school activity to showcase the dramatic talent of the students, put on for the benefit of the parents. On one of these occasions in particular, a student, a daughter of a well-known politician of the time, did a tap dance with another student from the high school. I was full of admiration for their skill and style. They were well-known beauties even then, and they grew up to become winners of beauty pageants popular at that time. Bathing suits were already being worn as the regulation costume for the judging.

It is surprising to me now that while I have no recollection of the other subjects taught and the texts used, I remember clearly that a thin Anglo-Indian teacher taught us scripture and catechism. We also had Domestic Science class, in which we made little aprons, and napkins and dainty handkerchiefs with threads pulled out at the edges and finished with hemming stitches. We learned to do some embroidery, too, of an elementary nature, like the cross-stitch and the making of tiny rosebuds at the corners of little square napkins. Studies were not a problem; my brother and I passed each standard with ease.

School uniforms were pleated navy blue tunics, worn with a belt and over a white blouse. Shoes and socks were also insisted upon. Bata shoes were the most popular brand. Each summer before school reopened, Mother would take us kids to the Bata shoe shop on the west wing of Scott Market to fit us into a new and larger pair of shoes. We used to look forward to the opening of school, when we could show off our spanking new uniforms and shoes and school bags – the only time, in fact, that they looked smart and clean. Heaven knows they get faded, dingy, and scuffed soon enough with the activities we got into each day at school. I never used to mind how I looked. I was the bane of my elder cousins at the same convent for discrediting them with my appearance, my tunic belt all twisted into a rope and the back of my skirts all dusty from wherever I had sat and played hopscotch and the Myanmar game of *Phan Khon* after school. But that happily was soon to change once Htut and I transferred to a coed school!

Chapter 10

Methodist English High School

I was eleven and in my sixth standard; my brother Htut, a year behind me; and Moe, in first standard when our parents moved us to the Methodist English High School (MEHS) on Signal Pagoda Road. Polay, the youngest, was not yet of school age. He joined the nursery class a year later, in 1952.

Originally, MEHS was founded on a different location and with a different name – Methodist English Girls' High School – with boys being accepted only up till the fifth standard. MEHS as we knew it in the 1950s was situated on its present site on Signal Pagoda Road and had come into being just before the war. It was run by American Baptist missionaries. Methodist English School, as it was then called, was situated right next to the Methodist English Church. British bombing during the last days of the war destroyed the school building, whereas the church survived. Dr Frank Manton as pastor of the Methodist church and chairman of the board of trustees of the school took charge of the reconstruction. Mrs Doreen Logie, who had been a teacher in the Methodist English School before the war, was made principal.

I do not know what prompted our parents to make the change, but one thing was certain: Htut could not stay on at St Philomena's Convent, which accepted boys only up till fourth standard. He would have to be moved. He could have been sent to a boys' school, such as the one at St Paul's run by the brothers of the De la Salle Mission, but the prospect of sending one child to a convent and the other children to another school might have been a problem for my parents. MEHS, on the other hand, was a coeducational school, so we could all be accommodated there.

The faculty was all laypeople, including our headmistress, Mrs Doreen Logie. The teachers were Anglo-Indian, Anglo-Burmese, or Burmese, and some Americans. And although they were strict, we felt they were nowhere near as rigid as the Catholic nuns. Corporal punishment was not encouraged at MEHS, whereas we always remembered feeling intimidated when seeing a cane in the hands of the nuns of the convent. Myanmar parents of children who attended MEHS served on the school's board of trustees.

Every morning there was an assembly conducted by the headmistress, where songs were sung and announcements were made. Either the music teacher or Mrs Logie herself on the piano accompanied our singing. The songs, "Jeannie with the Light Brown Hair," "Santa Lucia," "Waltzing Matilda," "My Grandfather's Clock," etc., were all popular. During the Christmas term, which was the term after the Thadingyut holidays and before the Christmas break, Christmas carols were sung. Although the majority of the students were Myanmar Buddhists, we all enjoyed singing the carols as well as the seasonal songs such as "Deck the Halls" and "Jingle Bells."

Class sizes were small, from a minimum of about twelve to a maximum of about thirty. In 1954 during our tenth-standard year, when there were two parallel classes, a bigger group of about fifteen were in the matric class. A smaller group consisting of most of our Anglo-Indian and Anglo-Burmese friends were preparing to sit for their General Certificate of Education (GCE), London University, exam conducted by the British Council in Yangon. The result of the examination determined if a student was eligible to pursue tertiary education in the United Kingdom or India. Of the few that I remember sitting for the GCE, there were Joyce, Prunella, and Matilda, who were such great netball and hockey players.

MEHS was a private school, registered as such under the Education Department of the Union of Burma. Our curriculum was approved by the government, so we were able to sit for the Government Matriculation. Passing the examination enabled us to go on to the University of Rangoon. I sat for the matriculation examination in March 1955; I was admitted to the university in June of that same year.

We all spoke English in and out of class; in fact, we were punished if we did not. Our Burmese Language class was the only class when we spoke, read, and wrote Burmese. Yet our standard was high enough for us to pass the matriculation with the rest of the students from around the country. Daw Ma Ma Gyi, our Burmese language teacher, was a brilliant teacher but a hard taskmistress. Once, her scathing comments about my attempt at an essay, using flowery and what I thought to be appropriately poetic language, left me traumatized.

We had a lot of extracurricular and co-curricular activities at MEHS. PE was varied and exciting, as some played hockey and some played basketball or netball, badminton, or tennis. Our annual sports days were held at the Aung San Stadium, which was once called the BAA (Burma Athletic Association) grounds. Girls as well as boys of our school played in and won the National Hockey Federation League tournaments. Our track and field was of a high standard since we had the long distance, the sprints, the hurdles, and the high and long jumps. MEHS track-and-field teams had won championship shields in inter-school sports meets.

Boy Scouts and Girl Guides were also popular movements at the school under the able leadership of Scoutmaster (my uncle) U Htwe Maung, who attended the twelve-nation International Jamboree held in the Philippines in May 1954. The school had also won the championship shield in elocution contests sponsored by the National Council of Women in Burma (NCWB) for winning three years in a row. The Variety Concert usually held in mid September, and the School Fun Fair held after that, were two of the most looked forward to events at the school. The school's journalism class under the direction of its journalism teacher was responsible for the publication of the MEHS annual yearbook, *The Swaying Palm,* which first appeared in 1955, the year that our class of '55 graduated.

Students were divided into four houses named after famous British and American missionaries and explorers. Thus there were the Livingstone, Carey, Wesley, and Judson Houses with the corresponding house colours of blue, yellow, red, and green. These houses competed against each other by gaining points on the basis of performances in sports, academics, special events such as the elocution contest, and extracurricular activities. Monitors or prefects from each class wore badges and patrolled the corridors, making sure that the students lined up quietly and orderly for assembly each morning, never ran in the corridors, and observed school rules.

I had forgotten what MEHS tuition was, so I asked an old classmate. He told me that tuition fees were K25 per month for an only child, K20 each for two siblings, and K17 each for three siblings at the school. And parents did not have to pay a lump sum; they paid by the month. I wondered how much teachers' salaries were. Of course, one has to remember that those were the days when a salary of K350 a month would buy a person a tical (16.40 grams) of gold.

MEHS grounds were beautifully looked after. By the side of the tennis court there was a big expanse of lawn bordered by flowers with, I think, a central showpiece of luxuriant cannas. There used to be garden competitions, and MEHS was the winner one year in the school gardens category. On the opposite side of the compound was a playground where soccer and hockey were played. This also used to be the area where school fun fairs were held. Basketball and netball were played in the assembly area, as was gymnastics.

One year there was a fundraising event for a new block of buildings. The strategy was for students to be given cards which had been printed with little rectangles to resemble bricks in a wall. Students had to take these cards home to sell the "bricks" at a kyat per brick to family, friends, and acquaintances. Once the bricks on a card were all sold, new cards were given. The students and families tried to outdo each other by selling as many bricks as possible. I don't know whether the students and their families raised all the money needed for the new building or if there had been other resources, but the new red brick building came up very quickly. At that time, my classmates and I were about ready to graduate from high school.

The fifteen students in our matric class were further divided into a science and an arts stream. In those days, nobody took private tuition in addition to classroom instruction, except for the one student who, even for then, was very focused and had very high ambitions. He would work long hours over his Myanmar language, searching for proverbs, getting their meaning, and learning how they had originated, since proverbs were always included in the matriculation exams as an essay topic. It was one of this boy's boasts that he collected nearly a hundred proverbs in his attempt to cover all bases.

The girls in my class, like Lily, Sheila (who had joined us only in the final year, having transferred from Darjeeling), Rosemary, and Shirley, were avid hockey players, very fierce in their games and suffering injury very often in the course of play. I can still see them during PE periods battling it out in the dusty field under a scorching sun and then coming back into class with faces red from being out too long. I couldn't understand their addiction to hockey under such circumstances. But the surprising fact was that these girls who were such keen sports players were also very good academically. Lily stood first and Shirley was fifth out of the whole of Myanmar in the matriculation examinations. Rosemary and Sheila were in the top twenty. Maung Myint Maung was the one boy who came out fourth. I never took to hockey for fear of being hit with the stick, which in the course of a game seemed to be whacked about in all directions, but I enjoyed playing netball. I remember Joyce for being such a strong opponent.

We girls often spent the day at each other's houses. During these times, we would just sit and talk, have lunch, or catch a movie together. But when we went to Shirley's place in Insein, we took our bicycles with us, as we would spend a lot of time cycling in the comparative quiet of Insein roads, which saw much less traffic than did the ones where we lived. In fact, we had the run of the road to ourselves as we careened around corners and pedalled up and down rolling gradients with abandon. This is not to say that our own roads around

Prome Road and Newlyn and Budd were too unsafe. We could still cross over the comparatively busy Prome Road, where our house was situated, to go bicycling on Fraser Road, where Winnie and Alwyn Tun Tin lived, and where the Shane girls lived. Winnie, Dinny Shane, and I were in the same class at school; since we lived close by, we saw a lot of each other. The three of us also got into silly teenage games like pretending not to talk to each other. Once, just for fun, Dinny and I decided to pretend to have fought and not to be on speaking terms. After some time of pretending, we became so shy about talking to each other that it began to frighten us. In the meantime, the gossip among our classmates was that we had fought over a boy! It was a good thing Winnie was there to vouch for us that we were only playing a game, silly though it may be. It was just that some girls were actually and seriously not talking to each other over petty rows. We were being very superior and thinking how stupid that was before the idea struck us to find out what it would be like. We found out all right.

Very sadly, Dinny passed away while still at school.

When our whole class was getting ready to register for the government-held matriculation exam, we all reverted to our original Myanmar names. Some took this opportunity to change their names from the simpler, old-fashioned one given in their *zartar* to a more fashionable one consisting of three words. The first two words were identical but followed the rule of naming according to the day of the child's birth, and the third word was matter of wide choice. We had whole generations of girls named in this popular fashion, I included. Thus we had Yin Yin May, Tin Tin Hla, Swe Swe Win, and so on. But fashions in names kept changing, so later we saw one-word names like Sandar, Thandar, and Ohnmar. Intriguingly, nowadays parents choose the most poetic names for their children, going back to Pali names or using names with five or six syllables, like Yun Pa Pa Wadi.

In 1965, after the military coup of 1962, the Methodist English High School together with all the other private missionary schools was nationalized. They metamorphosed into government-controlled state schools under the Ministry of

Education. The heads of schools were Myanmar, the teachers were Myanmar, and the medium of teaching became the Myanmar language. The schools were organized by township and were numbered consecutively. Thus MEHS became State High School (SHS) Dagon 1. (SHS) Dagon 1 continues to be a premier high school to this day, admission to which is highly sought after. The small Methodist church located by the side of the school, and the residence for its pastor, however, remains in the hands of the Methodist diocese.

After I graduated in 1955, the Methodist English Old Students' Association (MEOSA) was formed for its alumni, but MEOSA went the way of all associations when the Revolutionary Council came into power, meaning it was disbanded. I remember the many Executive Committee meetings held at my house when Thaw Kaung and Cecil Teoh were elected as presidents in turn. Shirley, Prunella, I, and others served in various capacities.

Methodist English High School Alumni (MEHSA), the brainchild of Juliet Teoh, came into existence as an informal association in 1987. The first ever international reunion was held in Kidderminster, United Kingdom, in 2001, when Mrs Doreen Logie attended in a wheelchair and met former students in an emotional reunion. The second was held in Los Angeles, California, USA, in 2006. The success of this reunion was responsible for the establishment of the MEHS Memorial Foundation in 2007. The last international reunion, the third of its kind, was held in Bangkok in January of 2008. The MEHSA alumni directory indicates that the majority of alumni reside in the United States.

MEOSA Executive Committee members after
a meeting at 66 Prome Road

Front row: May, Shirley, Prunella, and I
Back row: Ashok, Fred, David, Cecil, and Thaw Kaung

Chapter 11

Holidays and Weekends

While our trips by train to the hills were the highlight of our summer holidays, our December holidays had a different flavour. School holidays in December were one of the favourite times of the year. The skies were cloudless and blue, there was no threat of rain, and everyone appreciated the cool weather. It was time to see the annuals blazing in flower beds: the rich, silken colours of the phlox, the pale pastels of snapdragons, and the tall, stately hollyhocks. Favourite warm clothes were taken out of mothballs, picnics were planned, and it seemed to us youngsters that more than enough exciting events were crammed into this period.

There were the days leading up to Christmas, which, though we didn't celebrate the holiday, were always very festive because of our Christian friends. We often got Christmas presents and were invited to go carol singing or to attend an open house on Christmas Day. Then came the more exciting event, New Year's Eve. Before we were old enough to go to our own parties, our parents would take us to their friends' parties. There, old and young alike enjoyed the company, the food, and the singing of "Auld Lang Syne" with our hands linked as we stood in a big circle. We children enjoyed the novelty of staying up late and eating and singing until the countdown to the New Year. It was not a Myanmar tradition. In fact, we celebrate most joyously our own New Year on another date, but our colonial past had infused us with certain of English customs. In this case it was a happy one. It was just as well that New Year eventually came to be seen as an international event rather than a national one.

As if all these things were not excitement enough, we youngsters had the Independence Day parade to look forward to on the 4th of the New Year. This was the day when Burma gained its independence from Britain in 1948. And every year since then, it was a big event, one that we cherished and were proud to celebrate. The parade started from a maidan somewhere near Myoma High School and marched past the pavilion named the Bohshu Khan Mandat, which was right outside the president's residence on Prome Road, directly facing the imposing Shwe Dagon Pagoda. A cavalry detachment escorting the president's limousine clattered on the roads from the residence to the viewing pavilion early in the morning. Then tanks and cannons rolled past. Police on horseback and the soldiers holding banners, followed by a precision band playing rousing songs, led each regiment. The most colourful of these detachments was the Chin Rifles, as they came in playing bagpipes. The army, the navy, and the air force each had their detachments, and so did the University Training Corps. Women officers like Daw Khin Hla Thi would stand on the ramps of the tanks to salute as they rumbled past the president. The air force would salute the president with a fly-past in formation, in the shape of a *V* for Victory. My cousin Tin Tun, who was a pilot in the air force, flew one of the Dakotas.

This was the days of radio only, so we could not see the actual ceremony of the raising of the national flag in front of the president's house at twenty past four in the morning. But we knew it was going on. If we could, we would get up on the cold January morning to huddle together and listen to the radio broadcasting live from the ceremony. My brothers, augmented by the early arrival of their cousins, would rise not at 4.20, but they would get up early enough to make this a special occasion by raising a small national flag on the flagpole erected at the top of the balcony. All private residences flew them. It was an exciting sight to see the red and blue flags fluttering in the morning breeze right across the streets.

63

Even before the first light of day, the streets in front of our home filled up with people. We could hear the noise of their tramping feet and the chatter of their excited voices. After a hasty breakfast, we would join our friends living in the Halpin Road apartment buildings to jostle for a seat on the fence of the compound. There we would meet friends and talk, waiting in excitement for the first sounds of the marching bands on their return journey from the march-past in front of the president. It was both the spectacle of the parade and the fun and excitement of sharing it with friends that left a big impression on us. Parents of our friends would invariably have snacks like sticky rice or fritters to offer us when we went into their homes for a respite from the long parade or afterwards, when all the excitement had died down. We were loath to split up to go back home, so we would make arrangements for meeting later on to play tennis or ride bicycles. I remember that David Tin Hla was the one who was everywhere on his bicycle liaising among friends, finalizing this or that arrangement for us to meet again somewhere.

In the evening, our parents would go to the president's garden party in honour of the occasion. We children would be left happily at home with the thought of the final treat for the day, which was to watch the fireworks display from the balcony of our houses.

Whereas our weekdays were always busy with school and homework, our weekends were as exciting as a series of roller-coaster rides. There was always a picnic on the shores of the Inya Lake beneath a huge tree with gnarled roots, and the prospect of sleepovers with the cousins. There was boating and swimming in the lake, which was clear and unpolluted. There were very few other visitors, so we had the stretch of shore to ourselves as we frolicked and cavorted in the water.

Papa, Mummy, and the four of us children at Inya Lake

Since both our father, Aye, and our uncle Htwe were great swimmers in their days, this was something they encouraged their children to do. After about a leisurely hour or two in the water, we came out, towelled off, and changed into dry clothes out in the open. Then we sat down on rough mats to enjoy our picnic meal stored in stacked tiffin carriers.

There were more boys than girls in Aye's and Htwe's families with the boys predominating at a ratio of seven to two. The seven boys were within an age range of perhaps ten years. Just as Aye and Htwe were inseparable in their youth, so were the cousins. They went to the same school, spent holidays in each other's house in turn, shared activities such as scouting and swimming, and, when they entered the monkhood, became *koyins* together. It was only after they graduated, chose different careers, and got married that they ceased to meet regularly.

Back home after the swimming and the picnic, it was a continuation of the fun and games with only a change in venue. The adults, Uncle Htwe, his wife, Aunty Nu Nu, and our parents, would settle down to a game of cards or scrabble or mah-jong. This last always attracted our attention with its pretty little tiles with fancy writing or pictures on them. The shuffling of these tiles after each game was accompanied by a sustained clatter as they were whirled around with one or both hands. After some time, the maids would bring little trays of snacks and hot green tea or coffee, placing them on small side tables around the players. These refreshments the players would partake of as they continued in their play without interruption. In fact, any interruption was only very grudgingly permitted. And we children only came in to spy on the snacks that were being offered to the adults. As long as we were generously supplied with some for ourselves, we had enough diversions of our own.

Being the only girl in the family, I had to play "boy games." When I didn't feel like doing that, I would pretend disdain and go off to see what the cook was doing in the kitchen. Otherwise, I'd join the maid, who perhaps ironed the clothes with big copper irons heated with burning coals while she regaled me with stories made up, I realize now, to capture my interest. No real stories could be that engrossing.

I think it was only after Uncle Htwe passed away in 1958, at age forty-six after a massive heart attack, that my parents took up golfing and were smitten by the bug quite badly, so much so that we children became "golf orphans." While Father could play only on weekends, my mother was free to play throughout the week, which she did two or three times a week. Her golf mates were Aunty Amy Shane, Mrs Brady, and, later on, Mrs Kyaw Khine and others. They were captains at one time or another of the women's section at the Rangoon Golf Club at Danyingone. My brothers and I still have Mother's many trophies and medals won at the monthly and annual tournaments.

Up until I went to university, my social activities were in tandem with the rest of the family. We went visiting our cousins, attended each other's birthday parties and ahlus, and enjoyed picnics. One of the things I remember vividly as a teenager, when my parents promoted me to a semi-adult status, was being taken to the cinemas in town in the evenings. I was totally smitten by the glitz and glamour of Hollywood movies. I loved to see the likes of Deborah Kerr, Gene Kelly, Esther Williams, and Doris Day in extravagant musicals and romantic dramas. I remember one big African adventure, *Mogambo,* where Grace Kelly was pitched against Ava Gardner for the attentions of the enigmatic and moustached Clark Gable.

I also considered myself lucky to be old enough to savour the magic of the Myanmar stage in the days of artistes like U Myo Chit, his wife, Daw Khin Ohn Myint, and Daw Tin Tin Mu. No one can deny the enchantment of a stage performance. It is unfortunate that this special art form was extinguished in our Myanmar fine arts repertoire. It flourished just after the war when feature films that have been introduced before the war were not possible to produce because the film negatives were unavailable.

Aunty Nu Nu and my mother on their way
to a formal function

Chapter 12

66 Prome Road

Of all the houses that we lived in as a family, perhaps the one that stands out best is 66 Prome Road, although 58 (C) Inya Road replaced it once we had completed building it to our family's tastes and needs. Mother was lucky to have a large garden to work in after we moved to 66 Prome Road in 1952. Those

66 Prome Road adjacent to Pegu Club, belonging to the Burma Railways, and our residence from 1952 to 1965

were the times when properties, especially government-owned official residences, were at least one acre in size. Before that, in Hume Road and Fytche Road, as a more junior officer, Father was assigned only one floor of a two-storey house, which meant that the ground-floor residents and the upper-floor residents shared the garden and the drive. There was an Indian gardener, the mali, as we called him, looking after the quite spacious garden. I don't know how the sharing worked, but it often happened that only one party in the house took an active interest in the yard and the other was quite happy to let someone run the show as long as she and her children had full rights to pick flowers or run around in the garden.

My parents both took an interest in the gardening. Papa was particularly interested in the growing of vegetables, since he had as a child enjoyed growing them in competition with his other brothers in small beds assigned to each of them by their parents. But now he had only to specify what he wanted and where he wanted the vegetables planted. The vegetable garden was a sizable plot situated at the back of the house. The Indian malis were very skilled. They knew how to prepare the soil with organic manure, for which there were no alternatives, and which plants would grow best in shady or sunny spots. They were also very industrious, seeing as by dawn they would have started watering the plants from big cans made out of kerosene tins with an added spout of metal. These were strung to each end of a rod, which they carried on their shoulders. In the early evening, at about three or four, they would do another round of watering. Our favourite vegetables were cabbage and cauliflower, radish and lettuce, eggplant and ladies' fingers. My mother's eggplants grew big yet were tender and had a shiny coat of purple. They were such fine specimens that they were entered in the annual vegetable show.

In the cool season after the monsoons, our garden would blossom forth with tall hollyhocks, dahlias, and sweet peas, and low beds of phlox, dianthus, and snapdragons. And on low logs would be placed big wicker baskets of petunias, whose trailing vines spilled trumpet-like flowers of white or purple. Elsewhere in the garden there were bushes of star jasmines, which we loved to pick and string into garlands to offer at the altar. In the centre of the lawn, a bed of cannas blossomed year-round in brilliant scarlet and sunny yellow. In addition there would be a pergola-like structure where Mother hung her orchid plants under partial shade. And on the stone-flagged terrace, which ran right around the house, would be hung baskets of ferns and greenery.

Father also built a hen coop and raised a couple of dozen of White Leghorns and Red Leghorns. These were laying chickens. We children had the task of collecting the eggs and selling them to our neighbours who knew of our little enterprise and kindly patronized us. Dr Daniels, our railways doctor, was our favoured customer. We loved collecting the eggs and even feeding the birds, but cleaning the coop was happily left to our mali. Tending to the hens, however, turned out to be a passing phase among our many interests.

On the left side of the house beyond the driveway was a banana grove interspersed with guava trees where my brothers played at being the Banana Bunch in a small hut they had built. Most times during weekends and holidays, their cousins Htut, Zut, and Gut joined them. A huge banyan tree stood sentinel beside one of the gates. It was gnarled and huge. Squirrels made their nests there, and many a time baby squirrels would fall out of them. The chattering of the squirrels in alarm would be a signal that this mishap had occurred. My young brothers would run to pick up the baby squirrel and then try to raise it in a little box. But one time a little baby squirrel escaped and scampered about. In the melee of the boys' running feet, it was unhappily stamped on and died. The boys took it to the corner of the garden, dug a small hole, and held a funeral service for it, expressing their sorrow for the accident.

Right close to the back stairs were a mango tree and a *kathit* tree. The kathit tree, with its pale trunk, looked stark most of the year with few leaves, but at springtime it would burst forth with scarlet petals of brilliant hue. Then it would attract the mynah birds, which would make such a ruckus first thing in the morning. This then was the opportunity for my brother Moe to climb the mango tree beside the kathit, position himself on a branch, and shoot his slingshot at the birds. Any small bird he got would be taken to the cook, who was asked to pluck its feathers, clean it, and then fry it crisp. The rest of us who did not have a penchant for eating the small birds or the agility for stalking them would then lecture him, saying that the "mouthful of bird is liable to bring you a disproportionate chunk of hell." For some reason I don't remember my other brothers hunting the

I, at age twelve, play tennis at 66 Prome Road

birds. Polay had been a little chubby since the time he was young, so perhaps he was not too adept at climbing trees. Htut, who was a little older, was more interested in playing Red Indians or cops and robbers. I would join my brothers in playing whatever games I could, like rolling marbles or spinning the top or trying to hit a target with a missive slung from an elastic band – or just plain catch or hide-and-seek. But this was before I had learned to read well and was reading serialized romantic stories from the issues of *Woman's Weekly* that my aunty Cissy had brought in her steamer trunk when she returned from Edinburgh.

Uncle Gilbert, Aunt Cissy's husband, was studying for his chartered accountancy in Edinburgh. His wife and their young son, Stafford, were with him for a couple of years. Now Aunt Cissy had returned from a three-month-long journey by boat to give birth to their second son. Aunty Cissy was my mother's youngest sister and my favourite aunt. I have, since the time I was young, admired her grace, beauty, and kindly nature. She was the one who painstakingly made a fairy dress with lace and tulle for my six-inch doll. As I grew older into my teens, she was the one who helped me grow in confidence with her gentle suggestions and advice about clothes, grooming, and aspects of developing a personality.

Our Indian mali, thin and gaunt, and our durwan, Raja Pandi, who was a roly-poly figure, lived in the string of quarters at the back of the house. There were two sets of four quarters, wooden structures with a short flight of steps leading up to the rooms. The mali and the durwan slept and cooked in these one-room quarters. We children were on good enough terms for them to allow us to be there occasionally when they had their afternoon meal. This was rice and small dried fish, which were cooked in the hot ash and cinders left in their earthen stove after cooking the rice. Then they had dried hot chillies, of which they would take a bite now and then. Each had a tumbler of water beside his plate, and they would wash down their meal with this. Such was the simple and unvarying fare of these extremely frugal people. They had family in India to whom they sent most of their salary. It was estimated that Indians annually sent back crores of rupees to their families in India at this time.

From some unknown time before we had even moved into the house at 66 Prome Road, a family of Indian dhobis, or washermen, inhabited one set of these quarters. They had a huge, old bathtub which was always filled with water. They scooped out water from the tub to use it for rinsing the clothes after scrubbing them with a bar of soap then thrashing them on a slab of concrete. There was no powdered detergent at the time. Then the clothes were hung out to dry on the long lines the men had strung out in front of their quarters. The womenfolk took care of ironing these clothes with heavy copper irons filled with red-hot coals. Then one of the younger men bundled up the clothes in a huge, white cloth, secured the bundle on to the back of his bicycle, and went around delivering the laundered clothes to their clients. On the return journey, he would bring back another load of clothes to be laundered in this way. As a gesture of goodwill, the dhobis would sometimes render our family of their service when we were short of cleaning maids.

It was while we were living in 66 Prome Road that we had the most number of our cousins and aunts and uncles come to share the spacious two-storey house. Our cousins had come to attend college, or to spend school holidays while attending college and living in a dorm. Older cousins came in between job postings from one district town to another. And in one happy instance, my cousin Saw Saw, who was a few months younger than I, came from Moulmein to get married. She was seventeen, and she and her mother had come to spend the days before the wedding in Yangon with us. Hers was a "society wedding" at the Town Hall. She was married to an eligible bachelor of thirty, a ship's captain and a decorated one at that. The circumstances under which they had met and courted could have made the plot for a romantic novel. Nevertheless, we cousins, Khin Sann Yin, Khin Thann Yin, and I, were a little scandalized to learn that anyone could get hitched and settle down for life at such a tender age, given that all that filled the thoughts of me and my contemporaries at that time were clothes and college functions and boys. I was a sophomore at Rangoon University then.

The spare bedroom on the ground floor, as far as I can remember, always had occupants. Once it was occupied by my uncle, my mother's youngest brother. He was in the fledgling movie business at that time, working together with his elder brother, who was a sound engineer. One day they brought a camera crew over to shoot a sequence where the actress was indulging in a foam bath in the big tub in the bathroom. I don't know if that sequence ever got through and made it into the edited version of that film. For us children, that big bathtub was to pile into on a hot day and to have fun splashing water at one another with abandon.

The big living room at 66 Prome Road also served as a movie theatre. My uncles had projectors and films, and we would fill the room with rows of wooden armchairs with cane bottoms and watch such films as *The Three Stooges,* reels featuring Donald Duck and Mickey Mouse, and sometimes a sneak preview of one of the movies my uncle was involved in. Whenever one of us children had a birthday, our uncles would treat us to a movie show, in this way delighting our friends and cousins who had joined us to celebrate the special occasion. Polay, who later attended the Defence Services Academy with the intention of becoming a military officer, had in his childhood an unexplained phobia which made him run and hide under a blanket whenever a cartoon film was shown.

Right next to our house, separated by a barbed-wire fence, was the grounds of the famed Pegu Club. Dubbed one of the most exclusive clubs of cosmopolitan Rangoon in the days of British rule in Burma, it was a place where "wealth or attainment or character was irrelevant; only race counted," according to Maurice Collis in a telling commentary. It had inspired a cocktail drink called the Pegu Club, the fame of which persists to this day in bars across the world. It was a low, rambling wooden building with a terrace right around it, as was the case for most buildings of the time. There were about four tennis courts that adjoined our compound. Inside there were billiard tables and a bar. The flaming colours of a bougainvillea creeping up one of the club's white walls decorated the quadrangle. In our time, we watched movies on Saturday nights as family club members. And there were weekly dances when dance music from a live band would waft across to my bedroom window, delighting me with all the songs that I loved. No such frivolity occurs there these days, however, because the club had been turned into an office for the military in the 1960s. It now lies in disorganized neglect.

In the 1980s, Ne Win's government decided to use this prime piece of land on Pyay Road (as it is now called) to build the National Museum. Thus, the three fine-looking railways quarters for the three top managers were razed (in our time, the general manager, the deputy general manager, and the chief accountant occupied those houses) and a new, imposing building to house the nation's treasures was built in their stead. If such fine specimens of colonial houses set in large gardens had to go, one could not hope for any more prestigious an interloper in their place.

Chapter 13

Grandmother Goh

At one point in our young lives, our father's stepmother, whom we call Pwa Goh, became part of our extended family. Our elder uncle Bagyi Zin, since he had never married, accompanied her and was her constant companion. The two of them looked after each other and had a complementary relationship. I simply remember that at one time Grandmother Goh was not with us and at another time she was. She was a very stern old lady, not having much to do with us, just going about her own business and sharing only mealtimes with us children. Old people and the children ate earlier in the evening, while my parents had their meals later, after Father had come home from the office and played a game of tennis or relaxed in some fashion. As we sat around the table with our plates of rice for the evening meal, with the meat and vegetables in serving dishes in the centre, Pwa Goh, as the oldest in the group, had the privilege of serving herself first. She would invariably serve herself and then choose a choice bit of meat or chicken to put on her son's plate. After that it was a free-for-all as we children spooned gravy and meat onto our plates. There would be six or seven or even eight around the table, as we often had our cousins visiting us. When we got older and had families of our own, it amused us to talk about these episodes in our life when we scrambled for choice pieces of the curry in the serving dish that was set in the middle of the table for everyone to reach. Often the curry ran out before we had finished the first or second or even third serving of rice, at which point we would ask the cook for some more. At times we were lucky to be appeased, and sometimes we were denied. We were young and we were big eaters.

After meals and during any in-between times, Pwa Goh would bring out her shining brass mortar. It was about six inches in height, was shaped rather like a thin vase with an opening about two inches in diameter, had a pinched waist, and featured a base that curved outward. The tools that went with this brass mortar were a proportionately small wooden pestle, and a brass one with a cutting edge shaped like a chisel. This paraphernalia was used to prepare Pwa Goh's quid of lime-smeared betel leaves and areca nuts. She would place the quid inside the brass mortar, pound it down with the wooden pestle, and then cut it into small pieces with the sharp brass pestle. At the age of sixty or so when we first met her, she had teeth that were pretty bad and in no condition to grind the areca nut in the betel leaf. Using the brass mortar and pestle enabled her to eat the pulverized quid. This little ritual of preparing the betel quid and then cutting it up in the brass mortar was a great novelty for us children, the sight of which we would crowd around her to see. Sometimes, when she was in a good mood, we could persuade her to let us do the grinding for her. She might even let us go beyond that to make some betel-leaf concoction for us to eat ourselves. Almost always, we would have to spit it out immediately because it would make our heads spin.

Pwa Goh also had special apparatus for making her palm-leaf cheroots. The ingredients that went inside the rolled cheroot were also painstakingly prepared by her. There were tobacco leaves and stems, which had been finely cut up and dried in the sun. She got little plugs of paper ready-made from the market. The palm leaves had to be dried and pressed flat in a sheaf of paper. She made about twenty of these cheroots at one time. Every time she wanted to make a fresh batch, she would bring out all the items in little rolls and containers, lay them out on the bedroom floor, sit on her haunches, and start to make them, very quick and adept with the smooth, unhurried motions of her hand. The cheroots were then stowed in neat rows in a biscuit tin, ready for use. Smoking the cheroot and munching on Grandmother's betel leaf was to her what eating a snack was for us, sometimes because we were hungry, but more often because we wanted to eat a comfort food or to while the time away.

Pwa Goh believed that children should not intrude on their parents' hours of rest and relaxation or at mealtimes. She was very good at shooing us away if we should come to the dining table while the adults were having their evening meal in peace and quiet. Very often my parents would beckon us to come share some fruits or sweets, but Pwa God would invariably effectively bar them by saying, "Oh, the children have already had their share." But that wouldn't necessarily stop us. We went around to stand beside our parents, who then gave us a piece of fruit or sweet before patting us lightly on the bottom to send us on our way to our usual pursuits.

Some of the encounters between Pwa Goh, who was a disciplinarian, and the younger boys were not quite amiable. Once she had laid down a rule of such severity that it really got in the way of the imaginative exploits of my young brothers. But it was Moe who took it in his hands to wreak vengeance on her. Taking his small pocketknife to the wooden boxes in which she had stored her personal belongings, he hacked at them, leaving a string of cuts on the edges. He was discovered in the act by Pwa Goh, who followed him as he ran leaping over the boxes. He landed one foot in a spittoon that was placed next to the last box, upsetting its slimy contents. But that did not stop my brother, who easily outran Pwa Goh and escaped. But of course he did not escape so easily the wrath and the punishment from our father.

Pwa Goh, who had had such well-behaved sons, must have been stretched to her limits by the exploits of her grandsons, since it was not only my brothers but also their cousins who were such mischievous kids. They were never docile and were up to all sorts of scrapes as children. She was a stern and daunting grandmother, but she had always been kind to me; perhaps as the one girl among four grandchildren, I was a welcome change. She must have appreciated my relative quietness and docility. She was very solicitous when I started having period pains. She would make a sort of dark jam with aloe vera and palm sugar, and prepare herbal concoctions with ginger, to alleviate the sometimes excruciating cramps. The hot drink would send a warmth coursing through my stomach and make me feel better. She would also apply some sort of liniment and rub it gently over my stomach in circular motions. Her manner was, however, quite brusque in spite of her kind acts. I have a feeling that she had always been that way. She had been very good at bringing up her eight stepchildren, doing only what she thought best for them, unmindful of her own sacrifices. But one could expect neither sweet talk nor gestures of affection from her.

For as long as I can remember, Pwa Goh, with Elder Uncle Zin, had always lived with us or with Uncle Htwe's family. Pwa Goh had, however, spent the war years with Elder Uncle Yin's family in the district town in which her only daughter and son-in-law were also stationed. After the war, only Htwe and Aye were living in Yangon. Yin, recently posted back to Yangon, had very tragically passed away in a motor accident in October 1954. Tin was abroad, serving as a diplomat in Indonesia. Thwin and the eldest brother, Tha Kyawt, lived in Moulmein and in Mogok, respectively. When Pwa Goh died in December 1954, she had been living with Uncle Htwe and his family. His was a family of even more boys than ours and with just one daughter. Pwa Goh must have found that trying indeed. It was a different matter bringing up seven boys when she was much younger. Now, in her seventies, it must have been quite a different proposition. She stayed aloof. When one of the boys became particularly irritating, she punished him with her favourite form of punishment: a crack on the head with her bony knuckles. Once, the cousins had come for a sleepover, a common practice between the boys of Htwe's and Aye's families, and one of them was wearing Moe's little checked shirt. A little earlier, Pwa Goh was pretty annoyed with Moe for some reason but had not been able to catch him. Now spotting a small, wiry boy in a checked shirt taking a drink of water quite unruffled, she saw her chance and very smartly gave him a knock on his head with her knuckles, also issuing a sharp expletive. The boy turned, quite distressed and surprised at this uncalled-for admonishment, and she found she had got the wrong grandson.

U Tin Maung, as president of the Trusteeship Council, presides over the 27th session of the council at the United Nations Headquarters in New York, 1 January 1961

U Htwe Maung, as an accountant with the Burma Defence Army (later, he was chief accountant of the Municipal Corporation)

Chapter 14

University of Rangoon

Having attended a coed school had always seemed to me to give my female schoolmates and me an edge over our friends who had gone to a convent. We didn't feel shy with boys, and we didn't think they were such special, mysterious creatures. Our school experience had given us the confidence and the savoir faire to deal naturally with them. Not for us was the peeking out at the brothers of friends who had come to pick up their sisters at the convent every evening after school. Also, as so often happened, we girls were better at studies than were boys, admittedly at that stage, at least, we certainly had no sense of the male superiority. We felt we were better than boys were in many ways, unless of course one of us was so dumb as to have fallen over a boy romantically, or to have developed a crush, as we put it. If we were not afflicted with that particular ailment, and most of us were not, we sailed through our early teenage years of high school quite merrily and with ease.

But college was a different proposition. There were many boys who were much older, and they were not the well-mannered type of boys that we could regard as friends as naturally as we did other girls. They gaped and gawked, and seemed to find strength in numbers as they grouped in corridors and corners while the girls tried to walk past them as if running a gauntlet. Some of the boys seemed only to be looking for a chance to give the girls love letters. Most girls were smart enough not to take them seriously. A common gimmick was to borrow a book from a girl. Sometimes it was a notebook, which a boy would borrow under the pretence that he wanted to catch up on the notes given at a lecture class he had attended together with the girl. Sometimes it was a novel or a textbook. When the boy returned the book he had borrowed, the girl would find the love letter slipped between its pages. Some girls acted very dramatically when something like this happened. They would go and stand in front of the boy who had given them the offending letter and make a great show of tearing it up in front of him. Then the boy would find a way of giving the girl a sequel to the first letter, almost like a natural progression of events, accusing her of extreme cruelty in embellished rhetoric. If the girl were stupid enough, she would fall for it. If she didn't, she would have a rollicking time reading the letter with her friends and laughing over the extravagances of the statements. Still, these were the pretty harmless games coeds played at in my time.

Once in a while, there would be a flurry of anxious activity as the concerned parties received word that some boy was planning to abduct a girl as a last resort. There were some strange characters who thought they were living in the Dark Ages, thinking themselves justified in dragging off a girl of their fancy because they had no other way of winning her. During my time at Hteedan, I heard of two or three instances when such a thing was feared about to happen. I knew of one occasion when the boy did not make good on his threat, as that episode concerned a friend of mine. I didn't find out whether that was just a false alarm or whether the protectors of the girl were just very good at their job. But I also knew of one time when a boy did actually abduct a girl!

Hteedan was a special place that merits explanation. Yankin was its counterpart, and it deserves the same. When the matriculates of 1955 started college, we were sent to either Yankin or Hteedan, depending on whether one majored in arts or science subjects. We were supposed to stay there for our freshman year, which means we attended classes there for our intermediate in arts or science – IA or IS – as the case may be. Hteedan was a place in Kyimyindine named after the umbrella-making trade that was carried on in earlier times in that area. At the time when I attended college there, it was a row of dusty buildings in the midst of a poorer residential area of Yangon. There were some crappy, or so they seemed to me at the time, pathetic little huts which sold the usual *mohinga* or *ohno kaukswe,* and a tea shop where boys sat at small stools around a small table. Most girls, however, brought their own lunches in little boxes and went to an empty classroom, where four or five of them would sit around and share their meals with each other.

We students were assigned to different classrooms according to our combination of subjects. The lecturers or their assistants would emerge from the teachers' lounge and deliver their lectures at the appointed times. Serious students tried to get seats in the front benches, and those not so serious and willing to be distracted stayed at the back. The classes were not too big in size. There were maybe forty students at the most. The larger classes had around eighty to a hundred students. Sometimes we had to go very early to stake out our places in front, and sometimes there were fights among girls vying to be in the front benches. Admittedly, while there were those who wanted to follow the lectures seriously, there were occasionally some who just wanted to gaze on a handsome, young lecturer. One of these was a member of our group. The rest of us, who wanted to behave with more decorum, scolded her for it. She herself was all giggles and never gave a hoot. History lectures given by some brilliant teachers like Dr Than Tun and U Ohn Ghine were always packed. The lecturers had to call the roll to mark attendance at each class. In this way, we all became familiar with the names even if we didn't know the people.

In 1955, Myanmar had an elected parliament; U Nu was the prime minister; and his party was the celebrated AFPFL, or the Anti-Fascist People's Freedom League, which rose to power during the fight for Burma's independence. After a very short time, though, there was a split in the ranks of the AFPFL, and the student followers of these vying factions also fought for dominance in the Students' Union elections. There would be speeches on loudspeakers in the campus, and there would be leaflets flying around like insects. For some reason, these young men who harangued and gestured with such heated enthusiasm failed to arouse my and my schoolmates' interest. In fact, the opposite happened, and we were put off strongly. We always tried to get out of voting for either side, as the contestants inexplicably left us feeling completely antipathetic. Justifiably or not, we just felt that what they were saying was a lot of hot air. I feel sure that this attitude was quite unfair. But there we were, completely apathetic to student politics and to politics in general. It was ironical, therefore, that we felt terribly the denial of our right to vote for our country's leaders in our later years.

In our second year at university, termed Intermediate Part B, we moved to the main campus of the University of Rangoon. This, we felt, was the real thing. The campus was huge and old and was invested with the aura of past glory when compared to our makeshift cramped Hteedan quarters. This was the same Rangoon University where our parents had spent such memorable days and where historic happenings of such moment happened during Burma's struggle for independence. The buildings were big and imposing; the grounds were well laid out. We could drive in through the high, imposing wrought-iron gates on Chancellor Road and see Convocation Hall straight ahead, with its two mythical lions standing guard at its steps. To our right as we drove in was the university library; to our left, the halls of residence for men, including Ava Hall, where my father had stayed during his university days. There was the big Thitpoke Tree standing sentinel as it had done more than a quarter-century ago during my parents' time. The arts and science departments occupied the main buildings around a quadrangle beside the library. Our classes were held in what was then the Social Science Building, which housed the Department of Psychology on the ground floor, and the Department of Economics, Statistics, and Commerce in the rooms on the second floor. In 1964, when I was already on the faculty of the commerce department, this building became the premises for the newly created Institute of Economics.

On University Avenue Road and before we got to the main gates was the university's hospital, or sanatorium (as it was usually called), and the Students' Union Building, which was razed to the ground in 1962 by General Ne Win's troops for allegedly being the symbolic hotbed of student agitation and unrest. Indeed, it had been the venue where students like Aung San and Raschid and Nu had harangued British colonial policies in a continuing fight for independence in the 1930s. The University Post Office stood on the left, almost directly opposite the main gates.

Across the road from our Social Science Building was the Inya Lake, whose shores we students often visited in between classes to stroll along the grassy banks or to sit and talk under a shady tree. If we walked farther down, we come to the gates of the famed RUBC (Rangoon University Boat Club), with its logo of a green crocodile and crossed oars.

If we walked still farther down, we come to the gates of the equally famed Inya Hall, since the 1920s the dormitory for young women who attended Rangoon University. Although other halls of residence existed for coeds, Inya Hall became the iconic institution which university-educated women of Myanmar from many generations were proud to claim association with. Each generation of its inhabitants have their own special impressions and memories of their days at Inya Hall. Following are the words of my cousin Khin Sann Yin, who spent four memorable years there in the 1950s:

When I passed the matriculation exam in 1952–53 and decided to join the Rangoon University, I was given permission to occupy a room at the Inya Hall by its warden, Daw Thein Nyunt. Happy to leave the confines of home and the guardianship of my parents, I joyfully entered the life of a college student living in a dorm at the famed Inya Hall.

I shared a room with Khin Ma Yee, a fellow freshman. There I met and made many friends, among them Khin Khin Hla, May Than, Khin Khin Tint, and Shirley and Edith Archard.

Inya Hall faced the lake after which it was named and was built two storeys high in a *U* shape. It was not far from the building where we attended classes. After breakfast we left from the back of the Inya Hall and went to our classrooms. In the afternoons we came back for our lunch. After a rest we returned the same way for classes, from 2 p.m. to 4.30 p.m. Only students taking the arts and science subjects were housed there in Inya Hall. Medical students had a separate hall of residence. Coeds studied and discussed with classmates in the dorm's library and did private study in their own rooms. When we needed help, we could always ask for it from senior students, who regarded us as their younger sisters and were always kind and considerate.

We were allowed to accept visits from friends and relatives in the parlour from 4 p.m. to 5 p.m. daily. The Indian guard at the main entrance would send word when a guest arrived for one of us. We would check our appearance in the mirror, make ourselves pretty, and descend to the parlour to meet our guests. Relatives came but rarely; the more frequent guests were our admirers seeking a closer relationship. These were the friends we met while attending classes, at picnics, and at various other hall functions. They came to propose. While some were successful, some were given a knockout blow, which they received in dejection. In the first meetings, these male guests were received standing by the doorways and corridors outside in the hallway, but once they had been accepted as special friends they graduated to a seat in the parlour. This, then, was the venue where Inya girls met and accepted their life partners. It was a scene which has lingered in my heart after more than fifty years and still fills me with happiness.

The life partner I chose was a forestry student from the main university. I was a major in sociology and psychology. Since his and my classes were in the same building but on different floors, we would meet each other when going up and down the stairs. He proposed and I accepted. I found myself as if on standby duty at Inya Hall from four to six every evening for the next two years until we graduated and attended the convocation together in 1956.

At six every evening when roll was called and letters distributed, we learnt to connect the names to the persons concerned, and that way we found out who was who. We also found out which couples were tête-à-tête in the parlour. Of those couples, many have remained happily committed to each other in marriage to this day.

Many were the functions that our seniors attended. We freshers just looked on in envy. But there were others which were open to us. These were the Freshers' Welcome, and the Brain Trust and Debates at Judson Hall. Then there were the hall dinners, when sister and brother halls invited each other's residents.

In front of Inya Hall in the evenings, many young men promenaded and serenaded with guitars and mandolins. Others brought, in the dewy mornings, freshly picked gangaw flowers in season to present to their girls of choice, and yet others brought the less romantic but equally appreciated *akyaw sone,* a favourite hot snack for the girls. Some even risked the wrath of Warden U Hla Shwe to stealthily pick some roses from the Wellington Hall gardens.

The young forestry student that my cousin Khin Sann Yin accepted to be her life partner became, in the fullness of years, a professor in the Department of Forestry at Rangoon University, the director general of the Forest Department of the Ministry of Environmental Conservation and Forestry, and, upon his retirement from government service, the president of FREDA (Forest Resource Environment Development and Conservation Association), a non-governmental, non-political, and non-profit organization.

Throughout the 1940s and right on to the 1950s, Rangoon University (except when it was closed during the war years), was the most prestigious in South East Asia and was one of the top universities in South Asia, attracting students from across the region. Until 1962, when it was put directly under the control of the Directorate of Higher Education, a central government agency, it was operated by a council of professors, scholars, and government officials. Even in my time, during my bachelor years, there was a steady stream of exchange professors and students sponsored by the Ford Foundation. Professors from the American universities, alongside our own, American-trained teachers from Cornell, Yale, Stanford, Syracuse, and the University of Chicago, taught us classes in scientific management and sales and marketing.

Chapter 15

Carefree Teen Years

I was a freshman at Hteedan, the arts campus of Rangoon University, in my sixteenth year. College was a big change for me. There were hordes of people, of whom I knew perhaps a handful. Our small matriculated class from MEHS of perhaps fifteen students total had all opted for different subjects to major in: medicine, engineering, sciences, and social studies. The majority were in the Yankin campus, as they needed to take science subjects to become doctors and engineers. The rest of us were in Hteedan, except for one student who was part of the very first batch of students to study at the Defence Services Academy.

My first friends were people who attended the same lectures as I did. Then there were faces I became familiar with as I spent time in the Ladies' Common Room while in between classes. It was natural, perhaps, that out of these many friends, the ones that lasted were the ones with whom I had more contact in and out of classes, developing social relationships that reinforced the initial meeting. But for a time, my social circle remained one that consisted of my school friends, not the new ones I made at college.

However, that was about to change as college activities inevitably widened the circle of friends I made. I made friends at the university swimming pool, at the Inya Hall tennis courts, and at the annual regattas of the Rangoon University Boat Club (RUBC). Soon I was meeting these friends to attend parties, to learn the cha-cha and the rock 'n' roll dance at each other's

With Esme and Sonny during a
Thingyan lunch break

houses, to play tennis, and to celebrate the Water Festival at Thingyan.

I was a member of the Water Devils Swimming Club, which was formed by my brothers, cousins, and friends (most of them still at school at MEHS) with the encouragement of our uncle Htwe Maung. Jon, his eldest son, was a star swimmer at that time. All the young members, still in their teens, were good swimmers competing against the bigger clubs like the Mayo Marine, the Orient, and the Rangoon University swimming clubs. Our members practiced at the Inya Lake. Our association meetings were held on its shores in the compound of Jon's aunt, Aunty Sally, and in U San Lin's Union Bank quarters. When competitions were held at the university swimming pool on Pagan Road, I came across my college friends, who were always surprised to see me rooting for a small team other than theirs. My favourite competition was the water polo. Although our team put in a gallant effort, we frequently lost in that event to the brawnier ones.

Tennis for the women players at the university was usually held at the courts belonging to the women's halls of residence, such as Inya Hall. Sometimes men were invited to play at these courts. I remember one time when a young American coach was sent to teach the coeds to play tennis. They turned out in spanking white shorts and whirly skirts, all agog with excitement. The coach demonstrated the service, which was a crucial technique to be mastered, and had us all go through the steps: the positioning of the left feet, the slant sideways, the lifting of the ball, the swing of the racquet, and then the follow-through. But it was when we were made to play an actual match and we learnt to score it that we discovered the use of the word "love" to stand for a nil point in the game. All the girls were a-twitter when the young coach explained that *love* stands for "no points gained." And the team whose score was love against another team's score of fifteen, then thirty, and then forty stood to lose a love match!

As it did in the university days of my parents, the RUBC held its monsoon and annual regattas, invitations to which were much sought after by the girls of our time. Since we belonged to a group of friends whose brothers were members of the teams or were even captains of the RUBC, our group was sure to be invited. Harry Saing, Ko Kyaw Win, and Ko Tin Htut were all captains of the RUBC in succession, and we benefited as the friends of Sheila or Elsie or Kyi Kyi. Friends who were scattered in different faculties of Rangoon University were brought together at these all-school sporting events.

Dais, Kyi Kyi, Amy, and I at a Monsoon Regatta, 1956

But a new group was also forming in our midst and cutting across all interest groups. This group included tennis stars and rowing enthusiasts and swimming champs and some who were not sporty at all. The rage among this new group was dance. We met at each other's houses and taught each other to dance the jive and the cha-cha, for this was the fifties and Elvis Presley reigned supreme.

These dance parties, although accepted by our parents and our social circle, did not escape being branded as aberrations to our traditional culture, which looked down upon the "mixing" of the opposite sexes at such a level of physical intimacy even as a social activity. Our parents, after meeting our friends and knowing them to be the children of their own circle of friends and acquaintances, readily allowed us to have parties at home. In this way, they could even monitor, in a discreet way, these events. In such an open atmosphere of mutual trust, my brother Htut and I were free to join our friends for birthday parties, jam sessions, and get-togethers. We rocked and jived the afternoons or evenings away. We were, however, rarely late coming back home. Being late, by our standards then and by the rules set by our parents, was arriving home after midnight. Friends who did not have brothers as natural chaperones were at a disadvantage because their parents couldn't chaperone them and didn't trust young men to be driving home their daughters at such a late hour. Because of this, very often my friends would spend the night after a party with me at my house. Then it would be a special treat for us girls. We would prepare our bedding on the floor of my bedroom, get under a huge mosquito net, and talk the night away with relish and gusto until tiredness overcame us and our voices drifted away.

The most special group, one which formed a group within a group as it were, was the one that met for tennis at 66 Prome Road, our house from 1950 to 1962. Being blessed with a court in the railway quarters which my father had occupied since I was ten, I and my brothers, along with our neighbours – the children of U Shwe Shane, my father's colleague and friend since his Moulmein days – wielded a tennis racquet from a very young age, as soon as we could hold one. My parents and their friends and colleagues used to occupy the tennis courts, but as they slowly moved on to their game of choice, golf, we children and our friends took over the court. As young boys, my brothers started their tennis career as ball boys, as they were told that that was how they would pick up the game. Thus when my parents and Uncle Shane and Aunty Amy played a relaxed mixed-doubles set, or Uncle Tha Sin and U Thein Nyunt or Uncle Pe Maung played a high-powered singles game, the boys would be adroitly picking up balls at the net or at the back of the court and then spinning them back to the players.

When it was our turn to use the courts, the girls, including Doris, Winnie Tun Tin, and me, would play in the mornings. Doris would walk over from her house in the Halpin Road apartments and Winnie from Fraser Road, a road away. The boys, a bigger crowd consisting of my brother Htut; the brothers Tun Aung and Than Aung; and Harold, David, Alwyn, and Patterson, would monopolize the courts in the evenings. Only Patricia, who was a powerful player, got to play in a mixed tournament with the boys. Off and on, other tennis enthusiasts who normally played at other courts would drop in just to meet and chat with the regulars at ours. Thus in the evenings, if no other pressing need detained me, I was down with the boys watching their game and chatting with the others while the latter took a turn out. This is how we spent the fine evenings during the cool season, from October to February, when no rains were expected to mar the game. On Saturdays, this same crowd might meet again at a party where there would be music and dancing.

At that time, it seemed to us that this life of gaiety and freedom would go on forever, or at least as far enough into the future as we ever thought about. For to us then, the present was the moment. But already, reality and adulthood were nipping at our heels. We were finishing our college years at staggered intervals, as various degrees took different lengths of time. We became doctors and engineers and teachers at college, and some of us even got married! Doctors were posted to remote areas of the country. Some of us planned to go abroad for further studies. In September of 1962, I left my family and friends for a year of study at the London School of Economics under a Colombo Plan technical assistance scheme of the British government. Even though my absence would be for only one year, I felt that I could never be sure of how the plans and the dynamics of the relationships among us friends would change during that short period. But change it did, and the tennis group at 66 Prome Road was never the same again.

Patricia at the net, playing a game of mixed
doubles at 66 Prome Road

Chapter 16

Career Girl

My nostalgic visit to LSE in June 2000

I was twenty-three and working as a tutor at the commerce department of the University of Rangoon when I succeeded in getting a Colombo Plan one-year scholarship to study at the London School of Economics and Political Science. That was also the year, 1962, when the army under General Ne Win took over the reins of power in the country in a coup d'état that saw the first president of the Union, Sao Shwe Thaik, detained in prison and the prime minister and almost all of the top leaders arrested.

In the late fifties and early sixties, U Nu's government had sent a lot of young men and women to study abroad as state scholars, mostly to the United Kingdom but also to the United States. There were other programmes, such as that of the Ford Foundation, that of the Asia Foundation, the Colombo Plan technical assistance scheme, and the Fulbright Scholar Program, under which young people could apply to study overseas. In the commerce department of Rangoon University where I worked, as many as three or four of the young teachers had succeeded every year in their bids to study in the United States. Our professor and head of department, William Paw, had himself gone as a state scholar to study at Harvard and had finished his MBA programme there. Then there was a continuous stream of US-trained scholars returning to serve at the department.

In September 1962, I left on a British Overseas Airways flight to London. There was another student on the flight with me, but we were barely acquainted and so kept to ourselves on the way. I remember having to stop at Cairo and being amazed by the crowds at the airport and the babble of unknown tongues. I stopped to look in at a souvenir shop and found myself unable to resist buying a bracelet made of turquoise scarabs. It must have been a very common and cheap piece of jewellery meant for the untutored tourist, but it was so evocative of the Egypt I had read about that I decided I had to have it in commemoration of my having stood on Egyptian soil.

When I arrived at Heathrow, someone from the Commonwealth Office was there to meet me. This individual took me to a boarding house where students from other countries were also kept. The other student who had been on my flight had come on a different programme, a Burma government scholarship, so she was subject to different arrangements. We had gone our separate ways. That evening, I met and talked to some Nigerian students and then retired early to my room, in which small cubicle I spent the first strange and lonely night. My cousin Lily couldn't come until the next day to take me to her small apartment in East Ham. It was with real relief and pleasure that I greeted her. She, a resident at the Royal Eye Hospital in Surbiton, only returned to London occasionally. Somehow she found time to take me shopping for the essential warm clothes. She also fed me with home-cooked Myanmar food, which I was already missing.

The London School of Economics and Political Science (LSE), situated in central London, is known to be the only university in the United Kingdom specializing in study and research across the full range of the social, political, and economic sciences. It enjoys a worldwide reputation. Founded by Beatrice and Sidney Webb and George Bernard Shaw in 1895 as a city college, LSE has no separate campus. The main building stands right on Houghton Street. It is a constituent college of the University of London, which it joined in 1900. As one of the most selective universities in the United Kingdom, it is said to have the lowest undergraduate admission rate of any British university. It also has many international students as part of its student body. LSE boasts many notable alumni, including many world leaders, in the fields of law, economics, business, literature, and politics.

My year at LSE was remarkable in many ways. It was the first time that I had lived alone away from home; and England was the first foreign country I had travelled to. There were more Myanmar students than I had expected to see, and they became my senior colleagues from the economics and statistics departments when the Institute of Economics was formed in 1964. After classes, we all naturally congregated to the Shaw Library, each to our own corner of what appeared to me to be a vast room. For one thing, there was no one and nothing to go back home to at our digs; I think we were all lonely students in our own ways. For another, there was always work we could be doing. We would often meet for a tea break at one of the small corner shops that abounded. There we would talk and argue, for it seemed to be the fashion for students here to sharpen their locution and debating skills. The study of economics provided a lot of points to argue on. Once on a holiday trip with other students from my diploma class to the Lake District, I was holding a magazine to read on the way. The Englishman who sat on the seat next to me asked where I was from and what I was doing. On being told I was studying at LSE, he commented that he should have known from the magazine I was holding in my hands. LSE is well known for its liberal socialist leanings, since its founders were core members of the Fabian Society.

For my postgraduate diploma in a very down-to-earth subject, I had to do a lot of practical work in addition to coursework in industrial psychology and sociology, and management and organizational theory. My fellow students and I practised interviewing each other for industrial grievances, assessed each other's interviewing skills, and wrote term papers. Groups of us would travel on the suburban train to visit factories as part of our practical work. There were a lot of international students. I remember some of them as being from Pakistan, India, Malta, and Africa – also the United States. The host-country students all took a hand in seeing that we foreign students had a chance to see a bit of the English countryside and that otherwise we were not left to our own devices during school holidays. Our classmate Margaret McLennan very kindly took an Indian friend and me for a drive to the south-west of England on one lovely spring day. We stopped for a picnic lunch on a verdant stretch of farmland where birds twittered amidst nearby bushes. We later stopped for tea in a little church town, marvelled at its antiquity, and warmed to the friendliness of the local people.

The year in London was also the chance for me to soak in the rich cultural scene. I took advantage of every opportunity to sample the many diversions that London had to offer, such as shows and events that I had only read and heard about before. I chose an eclectic mix, as I had wanted to savour everything. I went to the opera; saw *Thomas Becket* at the West End; attended a concert of the London Philharmonic Orchestra; enjoyed the *Black and White Minstrel Show, Peter Pan on Ice,* and *A Midsummer Night's Dream* in the open air at Regent's Park; and visited the Tate and other art galleries that abound in London. For this I had mostly to thank a friend who had enough love of things cultural to spend the time and the money to pursue this interest and share it with me. I was indeed lucky to have such a breadth of exposure with expert guidance, and to discover in myself the same strong interest which carried me through in all the capitals of the world that I had the good fortune to visit later in my life.

Even closer to home, for an international student such as I, London House was a hive of activity. Out of the many clubs and assoications that existed, I was aware of just a few. I remember talks and discussions at the Goats Club every

Tuesday presided over by Miss Mary Trevelyan (later awarded the OBE). She took great interest in the members and would write to enquire when any of us missed a meeting. There was also a visit by the Queen Mother, who was a patron and in whose honour a concert was held. Among the performers from various international student groups, I danced to my favourite song by Daw Than Aye.

After the year was over, I was offered the chance to continue on and complete my master's degree. But my parents were against my staying on. They had let me go in the first instance only because it was a one-year stint. They now wanted me back. They missed their eldest and only daughter, and they were also concerned about me, who in their eyes was a young girl living on her own away from her parents. I came back, never questioning their authority to decide these aspects of my life; in fact, I fully understood their reasons.

My younger brother Htut, at the age of eighteen, had gone to England to study before I did. He had received a Burmah Oil Company scholarship and had gone together with four or five other boys his age. But a boy was different. Getting the opportunity to carve out a career was important for Htut, and my parents did not worry too much about him. With a daughter, though, other concerns apply; she has to be kept safe under her parents' wings as long as she is unmarried. So I came back to my job as a tutor at Rangoon University and to life within the orbit of my parents.

Upon looking back, I see that this was a very satisfying period of my life. I had the safe, cosseted feeling of having my parents look after my needs, which in a Myanmar

With Kyi Kyi and Anna (Khin Aye Pwint) as career girls, 1965

family came unquestioned, and at the same time the freedom to earn and spend my own money. I was able to give back to my parents in the form of a holiday trip and in other, small tokens of my love and concern for them. I even enjoyed the privilege of paying for my two younger brothers' tuition at school. This was the preparation for my role as eldest sister that my parents gave me so that I recognized my responsibility for my younger siblings. They in turn had ingrained in them a sense of recognition of their elder sister's authority over and concern for them.

Dais Zaw and Khin Aye Win (Elsie) in their graduation gowns in 1961

I visited Paris on my way back from London in 1963. It was a chance too good to be missed. My uncle Tin Maung had written to his friend the Burmese ambassador in Paris, H. E. Sao Boon Wat, to put me up for the five days I would be visiting. Their friendship was on such a footing that Mrs Boon Wat herself came to meet me at the airport and then took me to their residence at 60 Rue Ampere. Their eldest daughter, Susan, was away at school, so I didn't meet her then. I remember that Mrs Boon Wat took me to the palace at Versailles, and once on a long drive to the Loire Valley. I may have window-shopped a few times, but I don't remember buying anything; unsurprisingly, I had very little money. It was enough for me that I had a place to stay and my meals were taken care of. However, Paris was spoiled for me because it rained for most of the time I was there, which prevented what could have been more visits to many more places and the much anticipated promenades along the Champs-Élysées. The Louvre, of course, was a must, but I found it to be an overwhelming collage of huge paintings by hugely famous artists. The artworks were so numerous that I could not take them in or appreciate all of them.

Brenda, who was a student in Paris at that time, took me for an evening out, which is when I had the chance to experience the nightlife of the young and not so rich. It was after dinner when we went to what was called a *cave* (cellar), where young people mostly sat around, drank, smoked, and talked. I must have been very tame and dull company for the two young French friends of Brenda, for I neither drank nor smoked and I just listened to their talk, which I only barely understood. Besides, I had gotten sleepy very early in the evening. If I had been able to see the other patrons and been able to watch their enjoyment of the evening, it might have kept me alert, but the smoke made everything hazy and I could just peer into the darkness farther inside. But the excitement of going out at night and watching the cars as they sped down the wide avenues with their tail lights illuminating the scene remained with me.

It was a pleasure walking to the corner *boulangerie* with Mya, one of the residents of the house and with whom I shared a bedroom, early in the mornings for the breakfast croissants and brochettes. That remained a favourite memory of my stay in Paris, the delights of the delicious, thick-crusted, especially flavourful breads.

After Paris, I was on my own in Geneva. I took a shuttle bus into the city from the airport. I walked past storefronts and then sat on a bench gazing at the jets of water that played on Lake Geneva. Somehow I lost track of time and missed my plane to Rome. Because I had to take a later one, I missed my friends who had come to meet me at the airport. My hosts were my parents' good friends U and Mrs Thet Su, who were with the Food and Agricultural Organization (FAO) headquarters in Rome. Their daughters, Kyi Kyi and Jenny, one a little older and the other a little younger than I, were my schoolmates. I had to take a taxi to their house on Via Veneto. I still remember the smirk on the driver's face as he realized that with my unfamiliarity with the Italian lire I had overtipped him. He had certainly not expected such a sum from a tired, straggly-looking student.

Rome has always been for me a city full of sunshine and warmth since that first time. I also found it to be full of crazy traffic, water fountains, and fabulous statues. As first impressions went, it had stood out joyously from smoggy London and rainy Paris.

Back home, I reported to the commerce department of Rangoon University. However, a year after my return, in 1964, the Institute of Economics came into being. The Institute of Economics was formed in October of that year under the Union of Myanmar University Education Law. The new scheme was conceived to foster and build a system of education in the professions and technical fields, thereby providing the foundations for a new socialist state. Whereas previously economics, commerce, and statistics were independent units of study among other arts and science subjects, they were now to be integrated in a new field of study leading to degrees in economics viz. B.Econ. (Economics) and B.Econ (Statistics), plus the B.Com (i.e. commerce), which were already being conferred by Rangoon University.

U Aye Hlaing, who was a professor of economics at Rangoon University, became the first rector of the Institute of Economics, serving in that position from 1964 to 1975. The three major departments of the institute were put under the control of the following professors: U Tha Hto and Dr Maung Shein were appointed jointly as heads of the Economics Department; U William Paw, a Harvard MBA, retained his position as professor and head of the Commerce Department; and Dr Khin Maung Nyunt, a PhD from the London School of Economics, succeeded Dr Sundaram as professor and head of the Statistics Department. There was also a full complement of supporting departments in such disciplines as mathematics, English, Burmese, and geography. A newly formed Research Department was created in 1966 for Dr Ronald Finlay, who had returned with a PhD from the Massachusetts Institute of Technology.

I cannot leave off my account of the Institute of Economics without mentioning my research professor Dr Khin Maung Kyi, who had earned his doctorate in management from Cornell University after gaining an MBA from Harvard. He and Mrs Hla Oung were in charge of the postgraduate programme in the Commerce Department of the Institute of Economics when I and another faculty member were doing our master's degree work there in 1968. He, heaving thick, fat book under his arms, would come into the seminar room where we had our classes and fling the books across the oval table at us, with an injunction for us to finish studying one in a week and bring him back a paper at the end of that time. I still have a copy of Max Weber's *The Theory of Social and Economic Organizations* to remind me of those days. I mean to be totally complimentary when I say that Dr Khin Maung Kyi's classes were always nerve-wracking. Although I completed the coursework, I never achieved my master's degree, due to the time limitation set on the submission of the research paper. I was already in Yugoslavia and grappling with different issues by the time that paper was due.

Being a part of the Institute of Economics was exhilarating and intellectually stimulating. I am grateful to have worked as a member of a faculty which was made up of brilliant teachers and colleagues recently returned from such institutions as Harvard University, Cornell University, the University of Chicago, Syracuse University, and Stanford University in the United States; the London School of Economics in the United Kingdom; and the University of Ontario and McGill University in Canada. They had all come back to serve in their mother departments. There were ongoing research projects and interdepartmental seminars where a friendly rivalry among the three major departments was almost always in evidence.

As was fitting for a university, there were various social clubs such as those for the fine arts, classical music and dance, hiking and mountaineering, tennis, rowing, etc. Members of the faculty acted as advisors and were active members of these clubs. Many a time, there were musical evenings, weekend hiking expeditions, and tennis tournaments, during which friendships were forged among the colleagues. There were hall dinners when male faculty and students would be invited to women's halls of residence and vice versa, and male students would more often than not serenade the female teachers they admired with a rendition of a song made famous by General Aung San when he serenaded his wife-to-be. The art and drama clubs and festivals were a breeding ground for future luminaries. In fact, the Institute of Economics was a hive of activity, as was the main Rangoon University of which it was a part. There were activities – academic, social, and religious – too numerous to mention.

Terry, me, Khin Thein Thein, Maung Sa, Khin Ohn Thant, and Mary Ong, as tutors in the Commerce Department

Chapter 17

A Legacy of Love: 58 (C) Inya Road

Back in 1948, my parents were persuaded to make a property purchase together with their family friend Daw Khin Thet Tin and their long-time friends Daw Kyin Shwe and U Tun Ohn of a big piece of land leading off from Inya Road. The property belonged to Professor Pe Maung Tin at one time. At the time of purchase, it was in the possession of one Daw Nyo Yin. The plot must have been at least twenty acres, of which Aunty Daw Khin Thet Tin took almost ten and my parents took seven. That was in the days when Inya Road properties were mere thousands of kyats per acre. Aunty Tin's property was parcelled out in acre plots for her nine children and lay on one side of the road leading into it, and ours was on the other.

For a long time our plot lay vacant, except for basket weavers who lived in some squatter huts and whom we often visited to buy their wares. When my parents decided to build in the early 1960s, only about an acre plot remained for our house, as the rest had been sold off in nearly half-acre plots over the years as financial exigencies dictated. We children were unaware, and at least I had only a vague understanding, of the stresses and strains that were burdening our parents. Obviously, my father's salary as a government officer was not enough to support a growing family and the lifestyle that we maintained, which can be described only as comfortable and never extravagant. But, without a doubt, the last parcels of land that were sold were meant to pay for the construction of our family home after a lifetime of living in government houses.

It is true that my mother never had to work a nine-to-five job. She was a housewife; the word "just" never had any credence as a modifier for her title. She managed the household together with its retinue of domestic help, or so it seemed to me now, because there was a sweeper, a gardener, and a night guard all provided by the Burma Railways; a mother who was the cook and the daughter her assistant; and another maid. Mother looked after the children's needs, accommodated the many members of the extended family who came and stayed and went, attended to the many social obligations as a senior official's wife, and, last but not least, was a wife in the fullest sense of the word to my father. She was his friend, his helpmate, his confidante, his moral support, and the girl he had courted and won. My father handed over his entire salary to her each month and trusted her to make good use of it. But that also meant that she had to find means to supplement the income when it was not enough. I knew that over the years she had had to dispose of parts of her dowry of personal jewellery and off and on engage in sideline business activities that basically kept her at home. I can think of no better way to describe my parents' marriage than to

Mother distributing prizes at Rangoon Railway Institute for a billiard tournament

say it was equal and based on complete trust.

When house plans were being drawn up for the house on Inya Road, all of us were old enough to have a say in the design and layout. The young architect Khin Maung Yin drew us a dream of a house that nestled right into the landscape. The extensive decking all around the house reflected our penchant for living out of doors as much as possible, notwithstanding the rainy

Father, U Aye Maung, Deputy General Manager of the
Burma Railways in 1966

GM U Shwe Shane; Chairman of the Board U Kyi Win;
Chief Engineer U Yone Mo; Father; and his other colleagues
at the Burma Railways on an inspection tour

climate that prevailed for more than half the year. Some features of his design had to be sacrificed in the interests of security, but even so a house that had two separate wings, for living and for sleeping quarters, connected by an open passageway was a source of utter amazement to some of our friends. Not only that, there were tall glass doors from ceiling to floor in the living and dining rooms, designed to give a panoramic view of the outdoors. Beyond those rooms was the east decking, from which we could delight in the vision of the moon as it rose behind a curtain of waving bamboo fronds. On many a moonlit night, we had friends over for a musical evening or our family lounged on bamboo mats and savoured cups of Shan tea as we talked the night away.

I was away in London when the house was started in 1962 and completed in the following year. Since we were still in 66 Prome Road, the newly built house was rented out to the Soviet Embassy. But in 1966, by sheer good luck, we decided to move into it. I say that it was good luck because within the year, 1967, my father and another of his colleagues, representing the top management of Burma Railways at that time, were called in by the army colonel who was minister of transport and told they were retired from their jobs as of the next day. In this summary termination, devoid of any opportunity for proper leave-taking after a lifetime of service, the minister was just following the usual practice of his government. At least, because we were already in our own house, we were spared the humiliation and inconvenience of being kicked out of government housing. In fact, though, Father's fate was not an isolated case. It became a pattern that was repeated in many ministries as army colonels replaced the top echelons of the civil service, men who had worked for and qualified for their jobs through the civil service exams.

By sheer coincidence, my youngest brother Polay (Linn Myaing), who was attending the Defence Services Academy in Pyin Oo Lwin, was in Yangon and, at the very time our father was being given the shocking news, was on a tour of the Rangoon Railways Institute, of which he was the principal. When Polay returned home, our mother met him and told him not to be disheartened by the news that Father (aged fifty-two at the time) had been given his marching orders.

Our family missed the loss of a regular income, although it was not much. But our parents were comforted by the fact that except for Polay, a DSA student for whose education the State was looking after anyway, the three elder children had all graduated and were gainfully employed as either university lecturers or an architect with the Housing Board. We were not about to make our parents feel inadequate and pressured by this turn of events through no fault of theirs. We all rallied behind our father so he could adjust to this sudden change in station and enforced idleness, while we tried to deal with simmering feelings of injustice in our own minds. But in the end, we all decided to look on the bright side, which was that Father no longer had to endure the daily operational tussles arising from opposing points of view. Indeed, the new leadership regarded my father and those of his ilk as foot-draggers who failed to display the necessary revolutionary zeal. The grievance of the two officers who were let go, on the other hand, was that their honest opinions, when they went against the wishes of the leadership, were regarded as mere stumbling blocks on the fast lane to revolutionary success.

We had the best years of our young adult lives at 58 (C) Inya Road. We were able to discuss, expound on, and express ideas and viewpoints, to find and share humour in the daily vicissitudes, and to strengthen family ties through expressions of solicitude for each other. We were able to give undivided attention to our mother when she had a radical mastectomy, during which time we all pulled closer together as a family. My mother continued to play golf after her recovery, but she was no longer as strong. Plus, the expenses of the game had become a little out of reach. Besides, Father was at home all day, so she couldn't very well leave him to his own devices for the better part of it. Instead, they would have friends come over for a game of cards or just to chat and gossip whenever they were not otherwise occupied.

My father kept busy by involving himself in the improvement and maintenance of the lane where we had our property. The houses on Inya Theikpan Lane (as it was once called) at that time were few and far between. The houses were one- or two-storey villas (not the huge, colonnaded ones we see today) built well to the back of the large compounds. The gardens were spacious and graced with lawns, palm trees, and flower beds. And all the residents knew each other. When a twin ribbon road was built to improve on the original dirt road, my father took the responsibility of supervising the work of the contractors, walking up and down the length of the road as the work progressed. When we children went off to work in the mornings, we would see him giving instructions to the workmen while pointing with his walking stick, or leaning on it as he talked to neighbours on the lane.

Back in 1951, Papa had a nervous breakdown. We children never knew what had brought it on. I was twelve at the time. We knew only that my father had been sent abroad for a training course and he felt unable to go on his own without the company of my mother. Instead of going abroad, he had to take extended medical leave. During that time, he was slowly treated back to normalcy. I remember that the whole family went and stayed in Toungoo at the house of my elder uncle U Thein Yin to relax and enjoy a change of scenery and pace. Fruits and vegetables were fresh and plentiful there, and Father particularly enjoyed the oranges grown in the area. He recovered and thrived in the company of his brother, his brother's family, and his own family in an easy, relaxed holiday atmosphere. After a time, he started back to work, but my mother had to accompany him to the office. Eventually, that too ceased once he was back on his own two feet, but he sadly never felt the same complete confidence in himself again. His unexpected early retirement at age fifty-two, coupled with this breakdown, was felt by him as a personal failure. It returned like a refrain to haunt him the rest of his life.

Up until our teens, our father, at bedtime, made it a point to see us properly settled in, ensuring that the mosquito net was properly tucked in under the mattress so that it didn't get kicked open and inadvertently let in the mosquitoes. He would give us a smile as he peered in at us through the mosquito net.

That ritual had always given us a feeling of being cared about, of being truly loved. We would return the smile, turn over, and promptly fall asleep.

In our young adulthood, as we faced problems that came with burgeoning relationships, and new situations at college and at work, our father was always there to listen to us in a non-judgmental way. He would hear us out, tell us what he thought of the situation, and offer us suggestions. Very often we could come to a solution ourselves once we had been able to use him as a sounding board. And very often there would be nuggets of true insight and distilled wisdom passed on to us without our being aware of their import at the time.

In the early twilight, we often walked up and down the garden path or on the decking of our beloved family home at 58 (C) Inya Road until our mother called us into dinner. Or we might be walking off a full and satisfying meal under the moonlight while our mother sat in the shadows, smoking a cheroot. We could see its sudden flares in the darkness.

I think that all my brothers and I had this strong sense of a happy, secure childhood because of the way it had been brought about by our parents in the world they built for us, in the way they treated us and gave us opportunities, and in the way they related to each other with love, affection, and generosity. That had somehow bred a sense of trust and confidence in each other among the four of us. We understood and felt that this had been a supremely valuable gift to us from our parents. And that in turn was manifested in the way we tried to pass on this precious gift when we had children of our own. We tried to give them a safe and happy environment, even if not one of affluence, in fact quite the contrary. They would remember having to walk to school, rain or shine, walking to a grand-aunt's house to watch television when it was first introduced, and their mothers cadging a lift from a genial neighbour to go for their weekly shopping. My own children had in their formative years an absent father who had to go abroad to work after getting an early retirement from the Foreign Ministry. It was a decision of conscience on his part, one which we could not shake out of him. None of this had impacted adversely on our children's ability or will power to succeed academically, professionally, and in their personal lives. With the love and security that we nurtured for them in their childhood, we felt they would find fertile yet firm ground to strike their roots. And in the opportunities we were fortunate to be able to create for them in time, we provided them with the wings with which to fly far and high.

58 (C) Inya Road, which my family built and lived in for more than ten years during the young adulthood of us children

Part II

Of Roots and Wings
(1969-2005)

Chapter 18

Taw Ein: A Cottage in the Woods

After my marriage in 1968, at the patently mature age of twenty-nine, Ko Soe Myint (my husband) and I decided that we should start living an independent life as opposed to staying on with my parents at 58 (C) Inya Road as an offshoot household, benefiting from the established amenities of my mother. We would have been perfectly justified in taking this line of least resistance as a temporary arrangement, since Ko Soe Myint as a young officer of the Foreign Office was already slated for a posting to Beijing in the next year. But we were in agreement that we should be both responsible and independent in this start to our new lives. After all, we were old enough.

We had an eye on this little cottage named *Taw Ein*, which had been designed by an American architect, a graduate in architecture and urban design, who built and lived in it in the midst of a spacious Marian grove. It was a very much publicized structure since it was the architect's rendition of a native Myanmar rural

Soe Myint and Wai Wai Myaing, wedding ceremony at the Inya Lake Hotel in 1968

dwelling. The property belonged to our family friend Aunty Daw Khin Thet Tin, who had given this particular plot to her son Jimmy, also an architect, who had graduated and returned from Harvard. The cottage was vacant since the architect had left. The surrounding shrubs and creepers had overgrown all around it. But we saw the potentials. It was the cutest cottage that any romantic newly-weds could have hoped to find. Besides, it was just a stone's throw away from my parents' house. We could always go and have our meals there. We were going to have our cake and eat it too.

My parents took us to see Aunty Daw Khin Thet Tin at 82 Inya Road. She came out to see us in her loose, comfortable cotton clothes, with her beloved dog, Tony, trotting close behind her. She had been known to comb Tony's hair with the same comb she used on herself and to share titbits from her lunch or tea by setting down food on the saucer of her teacup. Now, she greeted my parents affably and the two of us with some interest as she tried to appraise what the young daughter of her young friend had turned out to be and to determine the calibre of her newly-wed husband. It was no problem for her to let us stay in the Taw Ein. No one was using it and, in fact, our habitation there meant it would be well maintained. She was happy to help us out. There would be no need for us to pay rent. We would just spend the amount needed to renovate the little house to our needs and taste. We came back elated with thoughts of turning the little house into our first dream home.

The cottage was an innovative wooden version of a typical Myanmar hut to be found in any village. It was on stilts and consisted of one big room. It had a fairly large verandah in front where one would leave one's footwear. This was appropriately called a *phinat chut,* in Myanmar. The windows had *ker lar,* or wooden flaps that were pushed out and up with a wooden stave to open them, and pulled down to shut them. The main door was made of folding wooden sections that were opened out or jammed shut with a stout rod going across them and held in place by two or more iron rings. The toilet and bath was a separate section at the back of the house, reached by a little bridge. A little lily pond decorated the area beside this bridge.

Now Ko Soe Myint and I set out to renovate the place in a way that the original owner was much better off not knowing about. We "modernized" the place in an attempt to make it easier to live in. We replaced the wooden ker lars with ordinary two-leaf windows. Ditto the main door. It became a two-leaf door with bolts and locks. We put in a partition for our sleeping area and created a bedroom and a partition for a smaller area at the far end of the room to make a pantry area. And, as an ultimate insult to rural style of living, we put in a Western-type commode and a flush tank. But we left the living room area free of any furniture except for mats that we put out for guests, and a small round table that we rolled in for our meals, thus keeping the Myanmar rural tradition. With running water and electricity, we had all modern conveniences. Taw Ein was a little dream of a house shaded by huge old trees.

In the rainy season, huge bullfrogs inhabited the small lily pond. Their booming croaks, which sounded like foghorns, kept us awake. Small "safe" snakes and poisonous ones infested the house, since we habitually left it unattended for whole days, coming back almost only at night after dinner at my parents' house. Only at weekends were we home whole days. Once as I went about cleaning the house, I lifted a tray of glasses to find a small snake coiled underneath. My spine tingled, however, when we found one under the folded blanket at the foot of our bed. Thankfully, and prudently, we had pulled off the counterpane and shaken out the blankets before getting into bed.

In the cool, dry season, which arrived round about October, we celebrated Thadingyut and Tazaunmon with lighted candles and strings of electric lights. We were happy to entertain our friends and family at these times. They all expressed interest in and envy of our modest yet delightful surroundings. Or perhaps they spoke with a touch of condescension for our decidedly modest habitat, but we were happy just to take their words at face value. We certainly didn't care if they privately thought otherwise.

But very soon after we had moved into Taw Ein, four months to be exact, family fortunes made it imperative for my two brothers Htut and Moe to move in with us temporarily. My parents moved into my uncle's house in the next road. Polay was in his last year at the Defence Services Academy in Maymyo. The little Taw Ein was then busy with the sound of people, since my father and mother spent their days there at Taw Ein and we had hired a maid who kept house and cooked and cleaned the whole day. We all had our evening meal together around that round table. It didn't matter that we were not at the "big" house as long as we were all together. We shared the days' happenings. I talked of my day at the Institute of Economics; Ko Soe Myint talked about the happenings at the Ministry of Foreign Affairs; and Htut talked about his exploits at the Housing Board. Moe was teaching at the Institute of Education but was about to attempt the Foreign Service exams. And with that many people and that much activity, the snakes were all effectively driven away.

The most exciting event that happened while we were at Taw Ein was that I gave birth to Aung Thura, our first son, at the Dufferin Hospital, later known as Central Women's Hospital. On my thirtieth birthday and my father's fifty-fifth, I was at the hospital with labour pains. I had been waiting since the day before in extreme discomfort and anxiety, but it turned out there was a complication and Aung Thura was delivered by caesarian section a day later. Aung Thura, as the first grandson to my parents and the first nephew to my brothers, was the apple of their eyes. Polay, on returning from the Seikkyee Naval Base, would be in a spanking white uniform and shining brass. On picking Aung Thura up in his arms, he would get smarmy little hands tugging at his bars. And Aung Thura's other uncles, Htut and Moe, would try every means to drive out the gecko (including spearing an onion to a bamboo stave and prodding the gecko with it) that lived in the ceiling and startled little Aung Thura from his naps.

Ko Soe Myint left Burma for his posting as second secretary to the Myanmar Embassy in Belgrade, Yugoslavia, in June of 1969. He went ahead to look for a house and have it furnished before I joined him with our young son. Houses suitable for our needs and liking, and at the rent the embassy allowed, were difficult to find in Belgrade in the 1970s. We also had to be prepared for living in an extremely cold climate where temperatures went below zero. Aung Thura, at eight months, and I left the little Taw Ein in September of that same year after packing and sending ahead a sea trunk filled with kitchen supplies, household ornaments, and our clothes. My parents then moved into the Taw Ein and stayed there for, as it turned out, only a couple months more.

A few weeks after my son and I left, my father developed a virulent flu and very soon afterwards found his eyes inflamed and causing him pain. Friend of the family and qualified ophthalmologist at this time Dr Myo Khaing was called in to diagnose the malady. He discovered that it was the dreaded glaucoma. He operated on my father successfully, but my father felt he had very little time left before his eyes gave out. He felt himself at a low point in his life and missed his daughter and grandson inordinately. Four months after the operation, his eyesight improved almost to normal and he started on his autobiography. He was fifty-six years old. The following is from Father's unpublished autobiography:

I direct this story to my first grandson Aung Thura and other grandchildren to come, their sons, daughters, and grandchildren and great grandchildren. My daughter and my three sons already know quite a lot about me, my sister and my brothers because my youngest son is already 22 years by the time I write this. But Aung Thura and future grandsons and their descendents would certainly like to know who and what their forefather was. Was he an aristocrat or a commoner, priest or peasant, labourer or landlord, superman or mouse? Was he a six-footer or a dwarf, was he handsome or was he ugly, was he bold and brave or was he a coward? They may want their forefather to be a tall, brave, handsome prince of the blood royal, and they may feel thoroughly let down by what they will learn about me from this simple story. Or they may feel happy to know that he was a man of strong principles and some accomplishments, and that he was quite a somebody in his days and it was not a shameful thing to own him as their forefather.

My father had started this autobiography on 26 January 1970, on the day his grandson celebrated his first birthday in far-off Belgrade, but never finished it.

Chapter 19

Cook, Maid, and Charming Hostess

As it turned out, Ko Soe Myint was posted not to Beijing, but to Belgrade, Yugoslavia. It was June 1969, a little more than a year after our marriage, and Yugoslavia under Josep Tito, leader of the Non-aligned Movement, of which Burma was a founding member, and of an enlightened communist state. Yugoslavia's people enjoyed the most freedom and prosperity of its communist neighbours, e.g. Bulgaria, Czechoslovakia, and Hungary, of that time

Josip Broz Tito created a federation of socialist republics – consisting of Serbia, Croatia, Slovenia, Montenegro, Bosnia, Herzegovina, and Macedonia – which lasted from World War II until 1991. He was the promoter of a policy of non-alignment between the two hostile blocs in the Cold War, and he was also the first communist leader to defy Soviet hegemony. He created a unique form of socialism that included profit-sharing, and workers' councils that managed the industrial enterprises, which was considered to have brought about the prosperity and the relative freedom his people enjoyed.

Ambassador H. E. U Thein Doke presents his deputy,
Soe Myint, to President Josip Broz Tito of the
Federal Republic of Yugoslavia, 1969

In Belgrade, which was Ko Soe Myint's second posting and my first experience as a diplomat's wife, we had to do a considerable amount of entertaining, as my husband was the second man at the mission. It was in a way an anomalous position, since he was only a second secretary. Compared to that, we had as our counterparts a first secretary from the Malaysian Embassy and a minister counsellor from the Thai Embassy. But in the diplomatic hierarchy, we were equal as the deputy chiefs of mission. Most of the missions in Belgrade of the 1970s were small, especially those of the South East Asian countries. The diplomatic community was also small compared to that of a place like New Delhi, which was to be our next post, and there was a lot of intermingling. We particularly became very friendly with the families of Ko Soe Myint's counterparts from the two missions mentioned above. We found we had a lot in common. We were all in our early or mid thirties with young children who were about the same ages as each other. We yearned for our own Asian food, which was similar enough that we could share meals hosted by each in turn with a great deal of anticipation and enjoyment. And we were young enough that the trappings of a diplomatic existence did not bog us down with its hauteur and stuffiness. We were, often enough, able to shrug off its foibles and pretensions with shared laughter and mirth and thus keep ourselves both grounded and normal.

Our Thai friend Aranya, or Khun Aranya as she later became, was an accomplished cook and hostess. Hana, my Malaysian friend, and I were, I think, both relatively new in the role, I more so. I was completely green. I had limited cooking experience and less hostessing experience, particularly of the type that is fit for diplomatic parties. Nevertheless, I had my husband's pool of experience as a young diplomat for five years in Washington, DC, and Emily Post's big, fat book on etiquette to guide me. In the same way, I had Dr Spock to guide me in my child-rearing. There I was, newly married with newly attained motherhood status, in a strange, far-off land assuming duties and responsibilities for which I was not adequately prepared. Whom could I turn to but the most authoritative people in print?

Although I had little experience with cooking, I had enough imagination and resourcefulness to be able to modify my native menu to suit the palates of our guests from various countries and cultures. There was no doubt that my dishes would be interesting, probably even exotic, but to make them palatable as well as look aesthetic was my main concern. The menu was, of course, dependent on the guest list, which was paramount. Ko Soe Myint and I would work over the social dynamics of inviting the second man from this embassy with the third man from that embassy who was of the same rank, and then someone from the Asian desk of the host country, and so on and so forth in various combinations. The guest list being settled and the invitations sent out by the embassy secretary, we would put our heads together again to work out the menu.

Fresh meat and chicken were readily available, but the fish was frozen and of a variety unfamiliar to us. Vegetables were also very limited, especially in the winter. All we could see at the farmers' market in the neighbourhood square, or piazza, were root vegetables like turnips and carrots. Cabbages were pickled and stored in big vats. I was fascinated to hear that the pickling agent the Yugoslavs used was bread, just as we used rice to ferment our vegetables. There was one supermarket I knew of where imported fresh vegetables were available. We mostly relied on tinned Asian vegetables like water chestnuts, mushrooms, and bamboo shoots. All these, in addition to the wines and liquor, were ordered through Peter Justesen, one of the import houses accessible to diplomats, from a catalogue. At one point, we even took to sprouting beans by ourselves just so that we get authentic ingredients for our Asian menus. Although the food was Asian, we adopted the Western practice of offering soup as the first course, followed by an hors d'oeuvre, then fish, and then the entrée of red meat or chicken accompanied by special rice. One simple menu, a favourite of ours, which we used with many variations on various occasions went as follows:

- Lentil soup mildly flavoured with spices and coconut cream
- Vegetable fritters or fried pan rolls
- Steamed fish cutlets
- Beef curry accompanied by buttered rice or fragrant rice
- Mixed vegetable salad and condiments
- Dessert: Semolina pudding

If we had Hindu guests, we added a chicken course as an alternative. There was lamb, but I was unused to cooking it and didn't feel confident serving it at our dinners. The semolina pudding was prepared three days ahead. I would bring out all the china, cutlery, and glassware needed for the party and have it rinsed and polished, and bring out the white damask tablecloth and napkins and have them ironed, two days ahead. The china, glasses, and cutlery at our house were government-issue. So was the ambassador's at his. Whereas the chief of mission entertained using china with a gold band around an embassy crest, our china was accented by a pale blue band. These were Noritake china from Japan. Over thirty years later,

I saw that same gold-banded china with the embassy crest in the middle used in my brother's ambassadorial residence in Washington, DC.

I resorted to cooking whatever I could one day ahead, and I left preparing only the vegetables and rice for the actual day. All these I would have to do single-handedly while my Myanmar maid stayed with my young son. Either that or she would help with the washing and cleaning up while I minded my son. The living room normally had to be left unadorned and bereft of ornaments and decorative articles of cultural interest for fear of the marauding hands of our toddler son. So on the day when guests were invited, I would have to bring out these items and set them up prior to arranging bowls and vases of flowers and placing them strategically. The first person to arrive, about an hour or two ahead of the invited guests, was the waiter who had been hired for the evening, bringing his uniform in an overnight bag. He would inspect the glasses, the china, and the silverware, and ask me about the menu and the order of serving the dishes. I would explain all these and show him the drinks that were to be offered before, during, and after dinner and the nuts, the dessert, the chocolates, the mints, etc. For the moment the guests arrived, I would not be lifting a finger.

But now, as soon as I had explained all these things to the hired-for-the-evening waiter, I raced upstairs, took a bath, and got dressed in elegant lace and silk. Then with my husband in a dark suit beside me, I waited for the first guests to arrive. We were punctual in Belgrade. Five minutes after the appointed time was when the first guests arrived. The waiter opened the door and ushered the guests in. I would accept the bouquet of flowers brought to me by one or the other of the guests and hand it over to the waiter. Whenever the sister of our ambassador in Belgrade was invited, she would send flowers ahead, and these would then already be gracing the unmistakably small living room. Very quickly, all our guests were ensconced in the deep stuffed chairs that were usual in Belgrade homes. I started with polite pleasantries to the guest beside me while the waiter, resplendent in white uniform and black bow tie, went around offering drinks, for my role as from that moment changed from that of cook and maid to charming hostess.

With Ko Soe Myint at the Hotel Metropole, Belgrade, on the occasion of our Independence Day celebration

Chapter 20

Life in Belgrade

Beograd, meaning "White City" in Serbo-Croat, has a climate that lays truth to that claim. In winter, the whole city is blanketed with snow at least a foot thick. The temperature goes down to thirteen degrees below freezing with the winds blowing in from the polar region. The river Danube that runs alongside the city lies frozen hard so that you can walk on it. In such weather, as I looked out of the bedroom window and saw the surrounding rooftops encrusted with snow and the ground all white, I felt myself occupying a shelf in a huge refrigerator, like a frozen fish. The sounds outside the house were muffled, and, except for the passing cars equipped with snow tyres, there was a strange silence.

We spent five years in Belgrade, suffering the cold winters with the help of the naphtha-run generator, and layers of woollen clothes when the generator failed, but rejoicing in the summers when we would visit the Adriatic coast. The beaches there were pebble beaches, and they were all crowded with people soaking in the sun while lying on towels or lounging in beach chairs. I have never known a people more intent on getting as much sun as possible as the Yugoslav people. One year we went to Sutivan on the island of Brac; another year it was to a small, rocky island on the Adriatic coast. It was an idyllic little island with pine trees and little donkeys carrying loads along the winding roads. We made friends with a local poet named Zoe Mamitzu, who was Polish. She invited us to tea and complimented Aung Thura on his impeccable manners, as he never forgot his "thank-you"s and "please"s. Nearby was the Brijuni Islands, one of which was President Tito's personal state summer residence to which many of his state guests were invited.

One year, Ko Soe Myint drove our sturdy little Volkswagen Beetle on a trip to the neighbouring countries

Ko Soe Myint with Aung Thura on the frozen river Danube

through Budapest, Vienna, and Rome, and right down to the tip of the Italian peninsula through Florence, Verona, Venice, and the world's smallest republic, San Remo. Budapest was two cities, Buda and Pest, with a river flowing between the two. We tasted the most delicious Sachertorte at a hotel patisserie in Vienna. Driving out, we got lost in the Vienna Woods. I had just been commenting on how romantic it was to be lost in such a place when we realized we had left our passports and our luggage at the hotel and got to bickering as to whose fault it was.

Rome we visited this time because Ko Soe Myint's cousin Nyi Nyi Than and his wife, Toni, had invited us to spend a couple of days with them and their two children at their spacious and elegant old apartment. Toni, a childhood friend, was daughter of U Sett Khaing, who was my father's colleague in the Burma Railways. U Nyi Nyi Than, after more postings to Beijing and Bonn, had reached the top of his career when he was appointed Myanmar ambassador, first to Indonesia and then to Korea.

H. E. U Win Pe, the Myanmar ambassador in Rome at that time, was my father's cousin. He graciously entertained us over lunch one afternoon. I was happy to see my college classmate U Zaw Win also working as a first secretary at the embassy. Rome had always been for me a city full of sunshine and warmth since the first time I visited, on my return home from study in London.

During the five years, from 1969 to 1974, that we spent in Belgrade, there were many notable guests to the Republic of Yugoslavia. Belgrade was honoured by visits from world leaders such as Queen Elizabeth and Prince Philip of the United Kingdom, Queen Juliana of the Netherlands, US President Richard Nixon and his wife, Pat Nixon, and President of the Republic of India V. V. Giri and his wife. As we, the foreign envoys, walked in line to present ourselves to Queen Elizabeth, we had to identify the country we represented. When my turn came and I announced, "Burma," the queen recognized me with a brief, "Oh, Burma!" – instantly making the connection to a former colony or perhaps to her cousin's title as Earl Mountbatten of Burma.

In those days, President Tito and his wife, Mme Jovanka, held lavish parties at the Federal Hall, which was graced by giant statues representing the six ethnic groups that made up the Yugoslav republic. There are many others of these visits I remember because Ko Soe Myint was chargé d'affaires ad interim during the absence of our ambassador, who was attending the UN General Assembly. The receptions, which went late into the night, were held in vast halls. It sometimes happened that we came home hungry after not being able to locate the rooms where refreshments were served. Dances by the ethnic groups were always the last event of the night.

My son, Aung Thura, started school at two and a half. I thought that was extremely young to begin school, but that was the recommended age for children to start at playschool. Given that Aung Thura was our first child, we were anxious not to let him fall behind in any programme of education and development. On his first day at the International School of Belgrade, I led him by the hand into the classroom, at which time the young Yugoslav teacher came forward to receive him. Aung Thura followed his teacher to a play area full of blocks and other stuff on the carpeted floor. He never once looked back. It was I who had to adjust to the new condition of being alone in the house in the daytime, not having him following me around with questions of why is this and why is that. He had the most questions of any child I had ever come across. He learned to speak Serbian with the Yugoslav driver, the secretary at the embassy, and the maids that occasionally came to work for us.

He was friends with a lot of young neighbourhood kids who were all a little older than he. They called him Antura, which sounds very much like a European name.

Belgrade also held unhappy memories for me, namely, the loss of my newborn baby daughter in a public hospital. I experienced complications in my second pregnancy in the eighth month and was rushed to hospital, where I was made to undergo bed rest for the rest of the term. But that didn't help, so there had to be a caesarian section, my second. I was told the baby survived for only a day. I was still recovering from the operation and the staff did not show her to me. A dull ache and an unexplainable apathy prevented me from asking to see her. Ko Soe Myint and my young son had the heart-rending experience of cremating the infant in the baby clothes I had chosen. The child's father placed a single pink rose on her tiny coffin. Back in Myanmar, my father had a dream that he saw a little girl in a frock. She had confided to him, "I shall not be staying. I am unhappy here." He was left with a strong sense of foreboding from this, albeit being completely unaware of what was happening. The hospital staff told me that little Theingi had been a beautiful baby. Hana, my Malaysian friend, came to the hospital to condole and weep with me. She and Imam had very kindly held a birthday party for my young son to make up for the absence of his mother during my lengthy hospitalization.

After I suffered through the tragedy of this loss, I was more than happy to learn of our impending departure for a new posting to New Delhi. I wanted to leave everything about Belgrade behind. We flew back to India in the summer of 1974, stopping in again in Rome, where Ko Soe Myint could not resist the opportunity to attend a performance of *Norma* at the Rome Opera House.

Chapter 21

Momentous Years

We had left Myanmar in 1969, seven tumultuous years into the country's experiment with the Burmese Way to Socialism under the Union Revolutionary Council headed by General Ne Win. Fledgling local industries like textiles, cigarettes, and soft drinks had all been nationalized after 1962, as were the banks and the insurance companies. Trading houses dealing in exports and imports were all wiped out so that the ever busy and crowded Scott Market (since called Bogyoke Aung San Market) became slowly a decrepit and desolate place with boarded-up storefronts interspersed with pathetic little stores selling government supplies. The Kengtung Store with its rolls of Tootal fabrics, Teejoomals with its imported silks and georgettes, and Bata Shoes – all shops that we had frequented were no more. The iconic Rowe & Co. premises were turned into a government office, as was the biggest indigenously owned department store, Sein Brothers. For now in our socialist state, all consumer goods were to be distributed through the PaPaKa, the acronym for the People's Stores, on a strict quota based on the size of the household and the age and gender of its members. However, the first few years of socialism were not so hard on us. We were still cushioned from its effects by the affluence of the recent past. Although imported goods were becoming a scarcity, domestic products were still readily available and relatively cheap.

In 1964, the Revolutionary Council issued a decree whereby all opposing political parties were abolished. A one-party system was established when the Burma Socialist Programme Party (BSPP) assumed complete control. In 1974, a new constitution was drawn up and put to a referendum. We were at the embassy in Belgrade, Yugoslavia. I remember going early one morning to the embassy to cast our votes. It was to no one's surprise when the referendum resulted in an overwhelming more than 90 per cent of the entire country in favour of the new constitution. General Ne Win dissolved the Revolutionary Council and handed over power to the Pyithu Hluttaw (the People's Assembly). The Socialist Republic of the Union of Burma was proclaimed. As U Ne Win, the general was elected president of the republic while still holding onto the chairmanship of the BSPP. With this mandate, he ruled us all, his countrymen, through the People's Assembly, which held supreme legislative, executive, and judicial authority. This was administered through people's councils at state, division, township, and ward levels.

Letters continued to arrive regularly from my parents, but with scant mention of the hardships and scarcities that must have started to plague them. For one thing, they were reluctant to worry us. For another, we knew letters abroad were being censored, and we couldn't risk letters not arriving. As it was, any delayed letter was waited for with bated breath.

After the tragedy of losing my second child at a Belgrade hospital, I was more than happy to learn of our impending departure for a new posting in New Delhi. I was also given permission for home leave at my own expense to see my parents again after five long years away from them. They were eagerly looking forward to seeing their first grandson, and I was just as eager to meet my new sisters-in-law.

After my marriage and subsequent move away from the family home, my three younger brothers had also started new lives and built families of their own. Moe was the first to tie the knot, with Julia, also known as Thein Thein Nwe, in April 1970. Ju Ju, as she is called at home, is the one and only daughter of Daw Khin Khin Maw and U Hla Aung, the latter of whom was at that time chief of division at the Ministry of Foreign Affairs (MOFA), the same ministry where Moe was then working. She had been born in New Delhi and spent her childhood there.

Wedding ceremony of Kyaw Myaing and Thein Thein Nwe
at the Inya Lake Hotel, 1970

Wedding ceremony of Htin Myaing and Than Than Ni
at the Inya Lake Hotel, 1972

Linn Myaing and Thi Thi Ta after the wedding ceremony
at 58 (C) Inya Road, 1974

Linn Myaing and Thi Thi Ta at their wedding reception
at the Inya Lake Hotel, 1974

Ju Ju went to school in Bangkok for a few years while her father was posted there. When her family moved to Japan, she studied at the Sacred Heart School in Tokyo from grade four until her high school graduation. She later earned a B.Econ in statistics from the Institute of Economics in Yangon.

Htut married Pyone, also known as Peggy or Than Than Ni, in 1972. Pyone, who had graduated from the University of Philippines in Manila, was the eldest among the five daughters of U Tun Thein, then working at the Economic and Social Commission of Asia and the Pacific (ESCAP) in Bangkok, and Daw May May Pu. U Tun Thein was a childhood friend of my father's when they were studying at St Albert's in Mandalay. He was also the younger brother of U Hla Aung, Julia's father.

Polay and Ta Ta were the only couple whose wedding ceremony was conducted in our family home at 58 (C) Inya Road. It took place in 1974. Ta Ta, whose formal name is Thi Thi Ta, earned her MSc in botany and is the second daughter of Sao Sai Mong and Daw Mi Mi Khaing, who lived in Taunggyi. Both of them were scholars and writers. Sao Sai Mong was the chief education officer of the Shan states, and Daw Mi Mi Khaing was the principal of Kanbawsa College in Taunggyi. Also, she had been a college friend of both of my parents at the University of Rangoon.

Sadly for me, the weddings of all my brothers took place during the five years when I was away with my husband and son in Belgrade, Yugoslavia. My parents, however, were blessed with three more grandchildren during this time. Tin Aung Myaing was born to Ju Ju and Moe in December of 1970. The two cousins Myo Htut Myaing and Mon Thiri Myaing were born nine months apart in the same year, 1974, to Pyone and Htut and to Ta Ta and Polay, respectively.

Our visit coincided with the unrest caused by the government's handling of the funeral arrangements for U Thant, our very own secretary general of the United Nations from 1961 to 1971. The populace, especially the students, felt that great honour should be accorded to this son of the soil who had made good in the international arena. They wanted to pay tribute to and accompany their beloved U Thant, "Architect of Peace," on his last journey. But the government denied him a state funeral for reasons of their own. This was just another instance of how far the government had removed themselves from the hopes, aspirations, and sensitivities of their own people. The people were suffocating from the repression under the socialist rule of U Ne Win and the self-imposed isolation from the rest of the world. According a decent funeral to U Thant, recognizing his contributions at an international level with an appropriate measure of ceremony would have asserted the country's link with the outside world, however tenuous.

For the mother and son on a short visit home, it just meant that we stuck close to home, something we were quite content to do, instead of roaming the city. But every evening, friends dropped in with tales of their efforts to show support for the beleaguered students who had seized U Thant's coffin and had placed it on a dais in the middle of the Convocation Hall. A neighbour came in one evening, tired but excited and said, "You should see for yourself what is happening out there. So many people like us. We handed in bunches of bananas and water bottles. Some were passing packets of noodles and fried rice. Others just watched and cheered. But the crowds were huge. We were so happy to get the chance to show how much we hate the military oppressors."

But this elation and sense of participation in a momentous event didn't last for long. Some bizarre turns of events took place when an attempt was made to bury U Thant at a mausoleum to be built at the foot of the Shwe Dagon and his coffin was seized by radical students who wanted him buried at the site of the old Students' Union. After three days, during which more crowds had gathered to cheer on the students encamped in the campus, riot police and armed soldiers stormed the university grounds. Shots were fired. Some students died, and some were arrested to face long years in prison. Finally, martial law was imposed.

Disheartened and with a sense of foreboding, we went back to New Delhi and settled in to an environment that offered more pleasant distractions: making new friends, trying out new foods, and acquiring mementos of a country in which we resided. Aung Thura started grade school at a conveniently located private institution. For me, there was another important mission, to provide my son with a sibling and to fill the longing in my heart for another child, a daughter preferably! When I wrote to my cousin Ma Ma Lily in London about my intentions, she wrote back, "Are you ready to face a third caesarian section?" I guess I was.

Chapter 22

Motherhood
(Second Time Around)

The most rewarding and satisfying experiences of my life were giving birth to my children, my son, Aung Thura, and daughter, Vasanti. For a woman, and speaking for myself, motherhood is a deep personal triumph. I must admit to having had some old-fashioned feelings of pride and accomplishment when nurturing a life of unknown potential within my body. As a first and an entirely new experience, I went through the course of a textbook pregnancy with Aung Thura. I suffered from loss of appetite and morning sickness the first three months, and I enjoyed rude health for the rest. After the baby was born, I suffered from post-partum blues. I was filled with anxiety and an unexplainable sadness. I felt inadequate to take care of the baby and was often in tears. With Vasanti, it was different. I was more confident, and I had planned for it. Added to that was the realization of my hopes and my dearest wish so long denied. The grief and despair of losing one daughter after my son was something I could never forget. I had hardly dared to hope for another child, let alone a daughter this time. But my sojourn in India had rewarded me with Vasanti, meaning "spring" in Hindi, and I shall forever be grateful for the conditions there which had made her possible.

Almost the first task we undertook after arriving in New Delhi, after the usual business of finding our feet in a new environment, was to ask friends and acquaintances about the conditions relating to having a child there in that city. In spite of our many happy times in Belgrade, our last posting, these had been overshadowed by the sad experience of losing my second child soon after her birth. My husband and I would not risk the chance of having it repeated. Everyone we met and talked to encouraged us and recommended to us the many admirable private clinics with their qualified doctors and requisite facilities. We were reassured. But feeling that a big hospital would be even more desirable in that it would own its full complement of up-to-date medical equipment, we began to consider the choice of a big hospital. At this stage, we were more than grateful to have our ambassador introduce us to a professor of obstetrics and gynaecology at a diplomatic party.

Professor Hingorani was the head of the Department of Obstetrics and Gynaecology at the All India Institute of Medical Sciences (AIIMS), the largest hospital in New Delhi and one of the biggest medical research centres in all of South Asia. It was also a teaching hospital. As such, its ob-gyn department handled only the rare and unusual cases that were referred by other hospitals in India. Professor Hingorani gave me a professional interview and, after hearing of my case and going over my medical history, decided my case was such as to warrant my admission to the AIIMS. I would be her personal patient. I came back very favourably impressed and with the fullest confidence in her as my doctor.

Once I came under her care, it was a case of regular medical check-ups and necessary medication. Nothing untoward happened, and everything went in the smoothest possible way. I took the utmost care and even avoided going on long trips outside the city. I took every precaution short of lying in bed all day. My two previous confinements in hospitals in two different countries had become associated with gloom and despondency I faced with dread another hospital stay. This time there was a difference: the stay was planned and prepared because it was to be an elective caesarian case.

I needed to feel no worries about leaving my young son and husband behind at home. I had inflated ideas about their need for me and could not dispel anxiety about their daily routines, including meals. I experienced utter dejection whenever I thought about their possible neglect. This time, with great good fortune, we were able to arrange a visit from my father and mother to coincide with my confinement. My relief was great when they arrived. So was theirs, because they had worried from afar about my third childbirth after the fatal second one. Travel outside the country was very difficult to achieve in those days of military rule, but my parents had been able to arrange it to their utter amazement and joy. As for me, I could now look forward in peace and contentment to my coming child.

On a mild sunny morning in March of 1976, my parents, my husband, and my son accompanied me to the hospital with its trim lawns and colourful flower beds and left me settled in a bright, spacious hospital room. Two days later, on a date of my own choosing, one day after the Hindu spring festival of Holi, I walked onto the operation table. Thirty minutes afterwards, my husband and parents were shown the baby, big and healthy with a head of hair all sticking out like fluff. The night before the operation as I lay in bed reading, dressed in my favourite flowery nightdress, a dazzling young Indian doctor in the most unlikely hospital attire of a flowing sari came with her retinue of nurses to check on me. On learning that I had a slight cough, she had ordered a medicated steam inhaler. I couldn't help feeling a tinge of envy of her svelte figure. She left me with a beautiful smile and a parting shot: "You are lucky to have the time to read that," she said, pointing to the two volumes of *War and Peace* which rested neatly in their case on my bedside table.

After the operation, as I lay in bed still groggy from the medication, my family received a stream of callers in the sitting area of the hospital room. The baby was brought to me and I gave her the first feed. If anything was to be remarked upon about this hospital stay, it is that it was the happiest and pleasantest I had the good fortune to experience. My doctor and Vasanti's paediatrician, the dietician and special nurses, and the presence of all my family had combined to make it so.

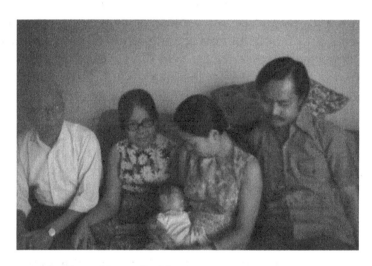

Newborn Vasanti with parents and grandparents
at Vasant Vihar, New Delhi, India, 1976

Chapter 23

Living in New Delhi

I remember vividly the sentiments expressed by Dom Moraes when writing about one of his brief visits to the Indian capital from his domicile in England. It echoed so closely my own feelings on the subject that I might have written it myself were I so clever. Transferring so suddenly from a Western scene, one felt that the stark landscape, the glaring colours, the teeming people, the heat, and the pervading culture had all to be remarked upon. It was unreal, our fortnight's stay at the grand Ashoka Hotel upon our first arrival from Belgrade, before a house was made ready for us. Because it served as a shock absorber, since a big hotel anywhere shares many similarities with the others, we wondered, "Where is the heat that people had warned us of?"

"It's not uncomfortable. It's bearable," or so we thought to ourselves in the air-conditioned comfort of the hotel room. But the magic of India was there, apparent even in the anaesthetized grandeur of the hotel, the dazzling arcades displaying silks and jewellery, the roomfuls of Kashmiri carpets, the rich embroidered woollen wraps and dresses, the resident palmist and astrologist, the bejewelled elephants that gave rides to the hotel guests every Sunday, and the tastiest, spiciest samosas and the most delectable mint sauce that had ever pleasured our starved palates.

Reality faced us the moment we set foot inside the small rented bungalow in a newly developed residential area, Vasant Vihar. The unrelieved white of the walls and the big glass windows devoid of any drapes or shades were unbearable in the blinding sunlight. The heat in the house as yet without air conditioning or coverings to keep out the sun seared the skin and left us parched. There was neither one tree around nor any foliage above four feet in height. The furniture that we had inherited from our predecessors, moved from their house and dumped now in our living room, was all dirty and dusty from the road. After the actual moving in, there was no one left to help us dust the furniture or set up our beds. And the prospect of cooking our evening meal on a kerosene stove lay before me. I felt ready to cry. I feared that in the burning heat of the room, the naked fire from the kerosene stove would cause the stove to explode. Of course it didn't, as I learnt after I got used to cooking on it. But that evening, in spite of our growing hunger, my husband and I decided to conserve our strength, so we lowered spirits to prepare our beds and be satisfied with consuming one bottle after another of warm soda pop.

That night, we lay breathless from the heat, sweating and tossing in the bed that was too uncomfortably warm in spite of the fans whirring overhead. We were just sleepless, but Aung Thura, our seven-year-old son, was delirious. I got up time and again to get him a drink. The temperature that night in June was 40°C. We had just two weeks ago left Belgrade at −10°C.

The next morning some friends from the embassy invited us to their home for lunch. We were never more thankful for a stress-free meal. They also found us a houseboy, Ashok, to help me prepare the kerosene stove for cooking, as I was still very fearful every time I had to use the stove, and to keep the terrazzo floors clean from the frequent dust storms. Another thing which filled me with inordinate dread and which needed getting used to and for which I found Ashok invaluable was turning away the numerous tradesmen selling everything from vegetables and fruit to cane chairs and embroidered linen. These people were insistent and aggressive and would not take a simple no for an answer. Nothing would do but for an imperious houseboy to turn them away with a "Memsahib ne hai." The moment they saw the mistress of the house, they would wheedle and cajole and almost plant themselves on the doorstep. With so many of them ringing the doorbell at all hours of the day, it became unwise ever to answer the doorbell myself. In time, however, the importunities were forgotten, faces became familiar, the supply lines became established, and an easy camaraderie set the tone between the *Memsahib* (mistress of the house) and the *subji*-wallah (vegetable seller) or the meat-wallah. I began to understand that I was expected to haggle over the price, to insist that the price at such and such a place was much lower, while the wallah, with an equal show of conviction, argued that it was just the opposite. After such an interchange, if the wallah still managed to put the price across to you, it was perfectly fair after all. If, on the other hand, you felt really cheated and thought a valued customer shouldn't be treated in this shameful way, you could rain recriminations on the man, who would take it all with a cheerful acceptance. But, oh, how time-consuming haggling was.

The dust storms in New Delhi were a bane to the housewife. Every year they would start around April or May, bringing the sands from the Rajasthan Desert and raging through at a furious rate, tossing high up into the air scraps of paper and any debris lying loose on the roads. The sky would darken with a reddish glow and then grow thick with dust while the roaring wind heralded the storm. The dust blown out this way, as from a giant inverted vacuum cleaner, would find its way through every crack in the doors and windows. Not even heavy drapes were able to prevent it from reaching farther into the house. A thick layer of sand would stretch across the floor at the edge of the doorway, and a finer layer would settle all over the rest of the floor and furniture. Since a brief thundershower invariably followed the dust storm, the outside of the house, the patio, etc., would become all streaked with mud. It would then be Ashok's task to wash away the mud outside with a hosepipe and to sweep and mop the terrazzo floors inside. A refreshing coolness the likes of which an air conditioner could never achieve was the aftermath of such a sandstorm and thundershower, and for this reason they were looked forward to, in spite of the work they created. A blistering day almost too hot to bear brought its own relief in the form of just such a sandstorm. But one of the perils of entertaining in New Delhi in the summer was the havoc that could be caused by sandstorms occurring just before the guests were due to arrive. The garden had to be tidied of broken twigs and scraps of paper, the patio washed down, and the dust brushed off the carpets and furniture; not the least of the worry was that the food may have gotten gritty with sand. Heaven help the hostess with gritty food.

After Vasanti's birth, with the presence of my mother and father in the house, I had the most contented and fulfilled time of my life. My son was seven years old now, and I was extremely happy that I had been able to give my undivided attention to him in his formative years. I now had the daughter I had longed for. My life was complete. As for my parents, every morning after coming into our room to see how the baby had fared during the night, they would take a walk around the neighbourhood, dropping in at the local shopping centre to see what was available and then bringing back a present or two for the folks back home in Yangon. Their last stop would be to a grocery store to pick up some vegetables or fruit. They made friends with the shopkeepers and found it very convenient that everyone spoke English with them. My father also had the opportunity to practise his Hindustani, which he had picked up from the many Indian employees in government offices during the time of the British occupation while he was in service with the Burma Railways.

With a newborn baby and in the increasing heat, I could not take my parents outside of Delhi to visit all the famous places they should be visiting. However, the embassy staff and the Burmese community there were very friendly and considerate. They invited my parents to meals at their houses and once even took them for a visit to Agra. I myself, in consideration of my delicate condition, had not undertaken any travel that involved long rides. For this reason, I left Delhi never having travelled farther than Connaught Circus and the Red Fort.

Once I was very pleased to have Daw Than Aye visit us bringing along Aung San Suu Kyi with her young son Alexander, who was about five years old at the time. I noted the sparkling eyes and the luminous skin of the young mother, but had no inkling of the monumental role she would later play in our country's destiny. Dora Than Aye, or Bilat Pyan Than as she was known professionally, was of the same generation as my parents, so normally I would have addressed her in deference in the Myanmar way as "aunt," but she preferred to be addressed as "big sister." She was full of confidence and had a positive outlook, and she brooked no denial of a fulfilling existence for everyone. Once I started a conversation with, "I wish I could do …" I don't even remember what it was I wished I could do, but she immediately pounced on me and said, "Why not? If you want to do this, you should be doing it." That was the type of person she was. On their return trip to Yangon, my parents managed to tie up with Ah Ma Gyi Daw Than Aye and stop over in Bangkok. They spent a few days together visiting mutual friends and paying homage at the Emerald Buddha. As a young girl, I very much liked her songs, especially "Mya Pan Ghway." The first song she recorded, it became an instant success. She later recorded many songs written by Shwe Daing Nyunt for Columbia Records. I used to think of her often, wondering where she was staying, whether she was in New York or London or in Austria. A few months back, quite by coincidence I asked my sister-in-law Ta Ta if she knew where Ah Ma Gyi Daw Than Aye was. Ta Ta did, and she also had her address. I asked for it, intending to write to the singer. She probably would not remember me personally, but she would remember who I was. But Ta Ta went for a short trip to the United States, having forgotten to give me the address. Very soon afterwards, I heard on the BBC, to my great sadness, that Daw Than Aye had passed away in Oxford, England. She was ninety-nine.

Chapter 24

Delhi Winters

It would be grossly unfair and unrepresentative to talk about Delhi summers without giving as much attention to its winters, which were glorious. They were sunny, mild (when compared to Belgrade), and clear. All the nicest things took place in this season. There was such a clean, crystal-clear quality to Delhi winter mornings. Nothing could be more pleasant than to enjoy a morning coffee and a chat with a friend amidst a garden ablaze with flowers. In Delhi, these were of the flower-bed variety, the annuals of delicate colour and gentle bloom. Their names – hollyhocks, sweet peas, snapdragons, and calendula – were straight out of an English country garden. Wave would follow wave of these flowers, since one crop as it died was replaced by another as long as the season lasted. And I could conjure up with pleasure one peaceful, contented morning I spent doing a watercolour of these tiny blooms. My young son was enchanted with the result. He came back from school and accorded it great honour by wishing to present it to his teacher.

The annual New Delhi Flower Show was held during winter at the Red Fort. Part of the fort was dedicated to the New Delhi zoological garden, which housed its famous white tiger (in 1978). On the other side of these famous ruined pink walls was where the flower show was held. The president's household garden also took part, with huge baskets holding fabulous arrangements of glistening carrots, aubergines, leeks, cauliflowers, and kohlrabies. Equally impressive were the cut-flower arrangements of long-stemmed carnations and roses.

Many embassies participate in this show. New Delhi is one of the cities which have the largest representation of foreign nations. Tulips from Holland and orchids from Malaysia and Singapore were flown in and, after the show, were sold at fantastically low prices. These lent exotic colour, but for me the scene-stealers were the masses and masses of Delhi flowers grouped according to colour. A circle of bright pink there, mauve here, glorious golden yellow in a patch, sky blue banked against scarlet, and so on. And among them all, flitting about like so many butterflies, were the beautifully sari-clad Delhites.

The President's House, called in Hindi Rashtrapati Bhavan, also throws open its Mughal Gardens to the public for a full one month during this time. Courtyard after courtyard boasts of its winter annuals planted in geometric design. The rose garden, which is considered one of the best rose gardens in the world, has varieties like Oklahoma, which is closest to being black; Paradise and Blue Moon, which are blue; and others from delicate mauve to deepest ruby in low bushes or tall climbers and vines. An arched passage leads through this scented garden down to the Circular Garden, where, in tier after tier of concentric circles, are planted a variety of flowers. The hum of bees rises up in the cool air and the mixed scent of the flowers assails the nose while your sight is greeted with a ripple of flowers growing wider and wider. And the majestic peacocks roam among them all.

India's Republic Day falls on 26 January. In my family there was always great excitement about this holiday because Aung Thura's birthday is on the same date. Pleasurable confusion reigned as we worked out with some close friends when we should celebrate his birthday party, which for a young boy of seven was still a big event. Should it be held the evening before in anticipation? Then there would still be the excitement of getting up early in the morning to take our places along Janpath to watch the Republic Day parade. The Presidential Guards, turbaned and scarlet-uniformed on huge stallions, followed the president's coach, which was led by a team of six white horses. The guards were followed in turn by other regiments, all equally impressive. Included were the floats, the artillery, and the local dancers of the six republics. All of these kept the children and adults alike in great thrall. At the end, a thrilling climax of six jet planes roared overhead to give the salute, climbing high and arching back in a great fleur-de-lys formation. Big plumes of smoke trailed behind them and froze in the cold January air.

The Beating Retreat was held on the third day of the Republic Day celebrations to denote the end of the festivities. Raisina Hill was the site of this moving ceremony, which was performed to the tune of mournful bagpipes and melancholy hymns performed by bands of the three wings of the military: the Indian Army, Navy, and Air Force. As the daylight slowly faded, mournful notes from the bagpipes curled into the air, a hush fell, and, for one moment as darkness descended, it was as if a curtain had fallen on the stage. Then one by one, ghostlike, torches appeared on the circular battlements, after which the hymns and the drilling resumed. Then, as the torches were extinguished and a final hymn, "Abide with Me" (said to be the favourite of Jawaharlal Nehru) was sung, the ceremony drew to a close.

Shopping was a delight in the winter. What in the blistering heat of the summer was a chore to be avoided wherever possible became enjoyable in the cool season. Whether you contemplated a walk down Janpath to do the obvious, or visited the brightly lit fashionable stores around the inner and outer rings of Connaught Circus or the crowded Chandi Chowk, you could gaze upon and linger at the beautifully embroidered Kashmiri shawls and the dazzling mirror work on household articles or intricate items of jewellery. There was a special place which housed salesrooms for products of each of the six republics of India. It was under a big circular dome. One could not finish going through the myriad of fascinating and fabulous items on display for each republic on one outing. Tamil Nadu was famous for its silks, Kashmir for its wools and carpets, and so on and so on.

After a tiring morning when my senses had become numb from the bombardment of such rich stimuli, I was ready for some refreshments. My favourite was this coffee place where you sat on high stools and could order the most delectable light, crispy, and huge (about a foot in diameter) masala dosa with a spicy potato filling. The espresso coffee was the perfect accompaniment.

Friends from the diplomatic community each had their own special collections from among this wide choice of arts and handicrafts of India. One Malaysian friend collected brass pots. Her living room boasted shelves of them in various shapes and sizes, filled with indoor plants trailing down in graceful profusion. Another friend collected famous pottery such as the Delhi Blue, made from a blue glaze formula handed down by artisans and craftsmen from Persia. Another friend just could not resist the travelling salesmen on bicycles carrying huge bundles of embroidered linen, some of strong cotton in white and various colours, and some of fine muslin; the choice was almost limitless. Those who had more money to spare would go for the Mughal miniatures, golden, gleaming, and sensuous. I was talking to a woman, one of the doyennes of the diplomatic community in New Delhi. Halfway through our small talk, I interjected, "My husband is very interested in the Mughal miniatures." I meant to say that he was but that I was not.

She responded, in a long-suffering drawl, "My dear, who isn't? The question is whether we can afford them." I realized right there that I had received a lesson intended for a green diplomat's wife from an old hand.

As it happened, my husband and I fell victim to the persuasive sales talk of a couple of tradesmen who were going round in a three-wheeler with a load of small items of furniture, little stools, side tables, and small coffee tables. These were intricately carved. Some were inlaid with bone or ivory depicting lovely Indian scenes: Gopal with the lissome milkmaids, veiled handmaidens frolicking in a garden, and so on. After an agonizing time choosing something which would be useful as well as appealing – and which fitted our budget – we settled for a small coffee table with a beautiful picture inlaid with bone. But it had to be made to order because we wanted something of a precise dimension with a particular motif.

The salesman listened to all our hemming and hawing and going back and forth with ideas with remarkable patience. He promised to deliver within the month, and we proceeded to pay the full amount for it. But the month passed, and two and three, and we finally ruefully admitted to ourselves our gullibility. Incredulously, we met the same group working another part of our locality while visiting some friends, and we greeted them as if they were long-lost friends whom we had longed to see. Indeed, we had longed to see them. We asked them why they hadn't turned up, and they gave a glib answer, which we accepted. We then extracted another promise from them to bring our table to us as soon as possible. This they readily gave and then disappeared from our lives altogether. Only afterwards we realized what we should have done, taken a substitute from them corresponding to the value of the money we had paid them. In fact, we saw and admired a small table with a chessboard carved on it, with a corresponding set of chess pieces. It was a tale of our complete naiveté with regard to the scruples of certain tradesmen in New Delhi. But we were not the only ones to suffer at one time or another from the crooked dealings of such conmen. We were, perhaps, the most remarkable for letting ourselves be duped twice.

Although I was not able to venture too far out of the capital, I was able to sample a few of the delights of living in New Delhi. There were the visits to Old Delhi and the teeming markets, which featured nuts and dried fruits of a huge variety piled high in the stalls; shopping at the city centre where each of the six republics of India had a big booth, its representative wares dazzling in their variety; incursions into the tiny shops selling the Mughal miniatures; the factories where the Delhi Blue pottery was made; and an enchanted evening when we went to attend a *kathakali* dance in a gracious old garden and to listen to the tabla, followed by a dinner of tandoori chicken and warm, fragrant naan in the company of our Indian friends.

Chapter 25

Half a House, yet a Home!

My parents kindly made room for our family of four in their Inya Road house when we returned home to Myanmar after five years in Belgrade and two in New Delhi. Our immediate housing problems were thus solved. But for our future, we had to make more permanent plans. We applied for a government housing unit at the Halpin Road apartments, the same housing complex with which I had been very familiar in my youth when we lived in the Burma Railways quarters at 66 Prome Road. My husband and I were unsuccessful, however. The thought of a downtown flat which was offered as an alternative did not appeal to me, so we went looking for a small house that we could rent in the residential areas. We were thoroughly dejected about the limited options we had at the rent we could afford, so we hung on to the room in my parents' house.

But that became an inconvenience and an impossibility for us and for them when they moved to a new house that was built for my brother Polay and his wife, Ta Ta. That was when we decided that we would build a shack, if it had to be one, on our own plot of land, which we had bought on our first wedding anniversary. That plot was fortuitously right next to my parents' house. We had found it with the help of my mother when she realized we were looking for some affordable property before we left for our Foreign Service posting. It turned out to be the place where my father took his early morning and evening walks whenever he felt the need for peace, quiet, and some contemplation. Reading through his diaries, which he faithfully kept, I can see how much that private place had meant to him all the years that it had stood empty while we were away. He had, moreover, with great foresight and *cetana,* planted many fruit trees and bananas in readiness for the day when his daughter would come back to live there. When my husband and I broached to my parents the idea of building on our land, they were more than enthusiastic. They would rather see us in a house, however modest, on a piece of land that we owned rather than pay rent on a small extension in someone's backyard.

So Father's carpenters and masons, the ones he had used for previous house renovations and projects, were called in. My brother Htut, an architect, drew up a very basic structure for three bedrooms, two bathrooms and toilets, a living room, a dining room, and a kitchen. Appreciating fully well our financial condition, my brother drew us a plan which would allow us to build half of the house for the time being, leaving open the possibility of adding to it and completing it when circumstances permitted. Thus it was that little Wai Sann Thi (the transliterated Myanmar version of "Vasanti"), who had travelled back from New Delhi when she was three months old, moved in to her very own home when she was two from Polay and Ta Ta's house, which they had graciously shared for over a year. How she cried that first night, saying she wanted to go back home to the only house she had known. Our very first home, our very own which we had built completely with the resources we had, was half a house. But how proud we were, and still are, of it. It cost us all of four lakhs in 1978.

That little half a house saw birthday parties for Aung Thura and Wai Sann Thi under the shade of a big tree in the spacious yard, and family gatherings and

The four cousins Aung Thura, Wai Sann Thi, Amara Thiri Myaing, and Mon Thiri Myaing at the half-completed 58 (E) Inya Road

meals for our friends from Thailand and Germany in the little covered patio we had extended on the side. We had also built a raised platform, a *kut pyit* that wrapped around a small tree in the garden for us to sit on in the evenings under the moonlight. Papa and Mummy could walk over for a visit of an evening, in fact, most evenings. And the cousins could come over to play with Aung Thura and Wai Sann Thi.

One month after our arrival, I accepted an offer to work at the newly opened Distance Education Department of the University of Yangon, which offered university courses through correspondence to the many thousands of students who matriculated each year from the government school system, the only one in the land.

I was lucky to be offered a job so early on and without having to go looking for one. The office was within walking distance, and the people I would be working with were from the university, a milieu I was familiar and comfortable with after having been on the faculty of the Institute of Economics for ten years before leaving it to follow my husband on his Foreign Service postings. The pay was what was commensurate for the post of a gazetted officer, which is above a post as a clerk. My salary amounted to K415, including a living allowance. It sounds paltry, and it was, but at least a serving of mohinga was K3, a *viss* (1,640 grams) of cooking oil was K36, one bag of rice was K140, and the weekly grocery bill was less than K100 at that time. Essential items like rice and oil were distributed by the state to government employees and the general public. When available, those were bought at about half the prevailing black-market rate. Every household had to be registered at the ward council and was issued with a ration book called the oil-quota book. Anyone old enough to have experienced those grim days will remember the ubiquitous and all-important *si-sar-oke*. This was the basis for the privilege of buying everything from toothpaste and soap to batteries, clothes, and stationery, in addition to the oil and the rice. When the *PaPaKa* saleswoman sent word that such-and-such a commodity was ready for distribution, someone from every household lined up or, more usually, crowded around to claim their quota. The PaPaKa saleswoman was someone who was fawned upon and whose hauteur and high-handedness was tolerated with resignation. She ruled the roost, so people tried to gain her favour.

During the time when Ko Soe Myint was working abroad for seven years, I would have been alone with my two young children were it not for Adawgyi, the elderly nanny who had looked after Wai Sann Thi since she was three months old. My friends now remarked on how brave I was to be able to carry on the way I did. But I had my parents, who lived two houses away, and, if truth be told, things were a lot safer back then.

That is, it was safer except for the time when Karen insurgents somehow infiltrated into Yangon and, unbeknownst to us, encamped in the servants' quarters of the house belonging to my parents (right next to ours), which was at that time being rented out to a young French couple. It so happened that the couple were back in France on home leave and the whole house was in the safekeeping of the Karen gardener-cum-guard. From accounts retrieved after the event, the insurgent cell had been in that house for more than a week. The first inkling of trouble we had was when there was a rocket-launcher attack on the nearby Burma Broadcasting Station and there were a few explosions in the vicinity. We had no way of knowing that these attacks were in any way linked to people who were trespassing on our property. That fateful morning, Wai Sann Thi, who must have been about seven years old, and I had gotten up early, about 4.30, to get ready to walk to the top of our lane. We were going to offer *soon* to the monks who came in a procession for their alms round, as was their custom every Wednesday. Just then, there was a horrific explosion alarmingly close by. We dropped to the floor and crept back into our bedroom, not knowing what to do next. Then there were shouts and a big commotion, and we saw soldiers marching into the house next door and coming out with armfuls of rockets and rifles.

It seemed that government forces had somehow traced the perpetrators of the rocket attack to this house and had surrounded the place before daybreak. Residents of the road unknowingly leaving their houses in the early morning ran smack into this ambush and were made to squat with their arms behind their heads. If we had been ten minutes earlier, Wai Sann Thi and I would have met the same fate. Or worse, we would have come face-to-face with the two insurgents who had gotten wind of the ambush and tried to make a breakthrough with a grenade in their hands. This exploded, killing them both on the spot and, in the process, scattering their limbs into the bushes on our private lane. The next day, the papers were full of the Mann Ngwe Aung Affair, as it became known.

Chapter 26

Tears and Laughter

.

In 1976, at the time my husband and I returned to Myanmar, my three brothers were family men with children of their own. Papa and Mummy now had five grandchildren to fuss over and worry about and to brighten up their daily life. This time when we were all together as a big extended family in Yangon was a happy time, although we were all counting our pyas and were charting our lives on the rocky road of the Burmese Way to Socialism. I was happy to have my sisters-in-law to share experiences and problems with, because every day living was always a challenge. We were all working wives and mothers, Pyone at the American Embassy, Ju Ju at the UNDP, Ta Ta at the International School Yangon, and I at the Yangon University once again. Thus we were all thankful we had our parents nearby to lend us support and bail us out of a tight domestic spot now and then.

Weekends were always family time at one or the other of our houses: at 121 Shwe Gondine, where Htut and Pyone lived (in her parents' family home); at Yoma Yeiktha, where Moe and Ju Ju lived (with her parents); or at 58 (E) Inya Road, where I, Ko Soe Myint, and our children lived. But more often we gathered where my parents lived with Polay and Ta Ta's family, at 58 (D) Inya Road. We celebrated our children's birthdays, shared Christmas dinners, revelled at the Water Festivals, and paid homage to our parents and elders at Thadingyut. For no other reason than that the weather was so gloriously pleasant in our cool season and the moon was full we would have *buthikyaw* parties out on the lawn. My trusted and patient cook, Daw Ngwe, with her beautiful, long hair in a bun high on her head, would fry gourd, onion, and banana fritters for us by the wokful.

All of us remember the times we rented a TV and video deck, collected three of our favourite movies (for old and young alike), and watched them one after another throughout the night. That was to be one of the most memorable entertainment programmes for us, one designed to bring us all together for a crowd sleepover at Pyone's house and at each of our houses in turn. A snack counter was conveniently laid out with a variety of contributions from each of us for intermittent raids throughout the night.

In 1978, Ko Soe Myint applied for and obtained a release from the Ministry of Foreign Affairs on medical grounds. I was worried and depressed at the prospect of an uncertain future with two young children to bring up. But for him it was a matter of conscience, and nothing could break his resolve; he would face working at whatever odd job if he could not land a regular one. In fact, he was for a few months driving a taxi!

Koyin laungs Zaw Zaw, Aung Thura, and Tin Aung Myaing
at the Shwe Dagon Pagoda with entourage
(grandparents, parents, young cousin and sister)

Aung Thura and Tin Aung
Myaing get their heads
shaved, with U Hla Aung and
Mon Thiri watching

During this period there was an event that was special and brought us as a family much joy. The two cousins Aung Thura at age ten and Tin Aung Myaing at eight, together with the latter's young maternal uncle, were ordained as novice monks (*samanera*) in a communal ceremony of the Mahasi Thathana Yeiktha in April 1979. In preparation, they had to learn the Pali verses that were to be their request to a senior monk (*Bikkhu*) of the monastery to allow them the robes and to ordain them. They then took up the Three Refuges, vowed to observe the Ten Precepts, and requested the teacher to be their preceptor. They were then given Pali names according to their day of birth. For the ten days that they were novices, they resided at the *yeiktha* and followed the rituals and routines set for such novices including going on alms rounds. At such times that they were invited to their own homes for the morning meal, they were treated with veneration by their parents and elders as exalted members of the sangha. Novitiation of their sons into the ranks of sangha is an event of great importance to Buddhist parents. When such an anticipated event is realized, it brings them much joy and rapture, as it did to Moe and Ju Ju and to Ko Soe Myint and me as well as to the grandparents.

In June 1979, Ta Ta gave birth to her second daughter, Amara Thiri Myaing, at the No. 2 Military Hospital on U Wisara Road, Yangon. That same year, Moe and Ju Ju left for their Foreign Service posting to Kuala Lumpur, Malaysia, for a four-year term. It was during this time that Moe was instrumental in bringing Ko Soe Myint out to KL to introduce him to a possible job opening at Universiti Malaya. He was offered a job teaching

Myanmar language at Pusat Bahasa, their foreign language centre, in 1982; he worked there for three years.

Since my parents lived in the house with Polay and Ta Ta, and since we lived one house away, four grandchildren were always around them. The three girls fought over who would pluck the stray white hairs from their grandparents' otherwise dark hair. They would fight over who would take their grandfather's hands as they walked up and down the garden path of an evening. Amara, the youngest, had the habit of biting anyone she was mad with. When this happened to Wai Sann Thi, she would go crying to her grandparents, showing them the marks of Amara's teeth on her arm. It seemed that the girls were jealous of each other only for their grandparents' affection, for they were amicable enough in other respects and, in fact, got on famously together whether they were playing hopscotch or marbles or zinging rubber bands with the brood of children belonging to the Karen cook at the American house next door.

During what I can only describe as the grim years of U Ne Win's military socialist rule, we hung together as a family, weathering the multitude of hardships that came in various guises. My parents would make repeated trips to the local People's Store to enquire about when cooking oil or rice would be available. Most times they would just resort to buying at the black market at several times the cost. They would send the cook to draw lots for an enamel bowl or a towel or some such utilitarian article. Once, they were allotted a half bar of Sunlight soap. My father's caustic remark in his diary was, "What are we to do with this, lick it for a month?"

Pyone gave birth to her second son, Tun Htut, at the beginning of our Thingyan festival in April of 1981. I remember how Ta Ta and I braved the water-throwing and took the bus to visit the newborn babe and the mother during the latter's confinement at the Rangoon General Hospital. Pyone was her usual cheerful self and was explaining how weird she felt going through the epidural. She said that while she had not experienced any pain, she was aware of every step of the caesarian section as it was performed on her.

161

Aung Thura, Wai Sann Thi, and I in front of the Pusat Bahasa, Universiti of Malaya, where Ko Soe Myint was working, 1984

In 1983, Moe, Ju Ju, and Tin Aung Myaing returned from Malaysia. The four of us siblings with our families were reunited back in Myanmar. We had made a short trip, the first trip abroad for little Wai Sann Thi, to visit Ko Soe Myint in his Petaling Jaya apartment, which was provided by Universiti Malaya. We were happy to have the opportunity to get in touch with our Malaysian friends from our diplomatic days in Belgrade and New Delhi. My school friends Kin Bo and Cynthia were very cordial, treating us to innumerable meals and taking us around in their car. Ko Phyu (U Win Thein) was a cousin of Pyone. We remember a very happy occasion when the former took us to the Genting Highlands and treated us to a delicious meal. While we were there, we received news of Papa's failing health. We spent the rest of our holiday with feelings of anxiety and apprehension while trying to make the most of our family's time together.

Ko Soe Myint's job first at the Universiti Malaya in Kuala Lumpur, Malaysia, and then in Bangkok, Thailand, enabled him to send us his savings in the form of four imported pickup trucks. That was the way things were done in those socialist days. Myanmar citizens obtained work permits and went abroad to work. They paid income tax of 10 per cent on their declared earnings and were permitted to import a motor vehicle. The cars were mostly reconditioned second-hand ones from Japan, but they fetched a phenomenally high price in a socialist economy where imports were restricted. The proceeds from those cars were enough, in those days, for us to complete the rest of the house. Htut's original plan was revised to make allowances for a growing son and daughter so they each had a bedroom with an en-suite bath and toilet. An altar room and a foyer were also added. Papa, who was ailing badly, was brought over by car, since he couldn't walk the distance anymore, to see our house in its completion stages.

The building-materials quota that was allotted to us on the basis of an approved house plan was not readily available. We needed to wait or else go through tedious and inconvenient red tape. The easy alternative was the black market, if one was willing to pay the price or was too pressed for time. What was not available, for love or money, were the fixtures and fittings, the little things that made the difference in a finished house. But there we were, owning and inhabiting a complete house after seven years of making do with half of it. Aung Thura and Wai Sann Thi now had a room each for themselves, but since Ko Soe Myint was still working abroad and I was alone, Wai Sann Thi did not claim her own room until she was well into her teens. Aung Thura, on the other hand, enjoyed having a room of his own and inviting his Teachers Training College Practicing school friends over for meals, karate lessons, and sleepovers.

My cousins Khin Nyunt Yin and Khin Sann Yin,
with their husbands, visit us at completed 58 (E) Inya Road

The four of us in the living room of our newly
completed house

A happy occasion when friends meet for lunch
at 58 (E) Inya Road – Anna, Kyi Kyi, Elsie, and their spouses

Except for times during the World War II years, my father endured the most difficult period of his life during the socialist era. He had gone through better times: as a child, as a university student during the colonial period, and as an officer in the Burma Railways both before and after Independence. After the coup d'état in 1962 and his subsequent premature retirement, he grappled with feelings of personal inadequacy. He also harboured a hopelessness about the country's economic and political future. He looked forward to a time when even such items as consumer goods would be freely available and not rationed out, when opportunities for his children to earn a living were free and plentiful, not limited to those postings as state employees, whose meagre pay was only adequate if goods and services were available at government-controlled prices, which they were not. It was obvious to see that rights and privileges were extended only to those in the ruling class, for a new social stratum had emerged. Its members shopped at special department stores, were given special permits to buy valuable and scarce building materials at government-controlled rates, and were allotted automobiles that were denied to everyone else unless one paid the exorbitant customs duties. Intellectuals started making comparisons to Milovan Đilas's New Class. My father never did live to see even the relatively improved new conditions after the socialist economic system was abandoned in 1994. "I don't think this government is ever going to change. However much I want to see their downfall, I think I shall be the one to depart the scene first" was his disheartened cry. His words, sadly, proved true.

I am happy to say, however, that in Father's last years he seemed to have come to peace with all such human failings in himself and others, thanks to his increasing understanding and embracing of Buddha's dhamma. He meditated and read a lot of the Mogok Dhamma, underlining the salient points in the book, noting down the dates on which he read the passages, and coming back again and again to the parts that particularly impressed him. In the few years before his illness, the occasions he most looked forward to were the dhamma meetings that were held regularly and among a group of like-minded friends. This group held communal prayers and shared merit and discussed various aspects of Buddhist teachings. Father gave me the special task of arranging the lunch that was served when it was his turn to host the event. He would go over the menu and give particular instructions as to the preparation of the main items. He wanted to be sure his friends, mostly all of advanced ages, would be able to enjoy the meal.

My father passed away in January 1985 after almost two years of a slowly debilitating disease of the liver. He grew painfully thin, and his skin got dark and dry. At first, before we found out the cause, his complaint was that he could not digest well. He who had loved to eat heartily with his children and grandchildren around him was reduced to sitting out while he watched the rest of us enjoying the meal my mother had cooked. She was an excellent cook who loved to cook for all of us.

My mother, who had taken care of my father all through his lengthy illness, was overwrought and in anguish when he finally drew his last breath on the hospital bed at the Defence Services General Hospital. She threw herself on his chest and cried, *"Kyay nat par, Aye yer,"* beseeching him to understand that she had cared for him as best she could.

In June 1987, I resigned from my post at the Distance Education Department of the University of Yangon and joined the International School Rangoon (ISR) as administrative assistant to the director of the school. A very small school at that time, it was situated on a residential property at 61 Insein Road, with an enrolment of about eighty students from nursery to grade eight. It moved to its present site at 20 Golden Valley in June 1988, just before the countrywide political upheaval in August of that same year.

Chapter 27

Clearer Waters and Greener Pastures

In April 1988 when Wai Sann Thi was twelve, she and a few other school friends decided that they would like to enter a nunnery during their school holidays. My husband and I were a little surprised and delighted that they had come to the decision on their own initiative. After all, they were going to

Wai Sann Thi and Sandhi Aung in ceremonial dress in a pre-novitiation event

have religious instruction and training and be introduced to the disciplined life of a Buddhist nun. This would give them a good, strong foundation of faith and piety to prepare them for life. I myself had never contemplated this selfless existence, not even for a short period, during my youth. The very act of shaving off one's hair signified the discarding of vanity, self-indulgence, and frivolity. I was full of admiration for my daughter's resolve. Her grandmother, grand-aunts, aunts, and friends attended her novitiation ceremony at the Nyana Sari Monastery, where she and her fellow novitiates had spent seven edifying days.

Novice Wunna Theingi with her mother, grandmother, aunts, and friends

In contrast to this peaceful and propitious event in our private lives, the country as a whole was in a state of growing turmoil. There were economic crises. A series of demonetization of banknotes in the currency led to the impoverishment of many of the people. In December 1987, the United Nations assigned Myanmar a status of least developed country. It seemed to be the last straw for the Myanmar people. On 8 August 1988, widespread protests and demonstrations broke out. These seemed to be made up of people from all walks of life; students, housewives, peasants, government employees, and artists all participated in increasing numbers. This state of affairs was triggered directly by the brutal police repression of the student-led protests, which had ended with hundreds of students and civilians being killed a few months earlier, and indirectly by years of growing discontent. On 18 September 1988, the State Law and Order Restoration Council (SLORC) took over the reins of government, with General Saw Maung as the chairman.

The most socially distressing aspect of the times for the country as a whole, and one that gave us the most concern, was the instability of the educational system and its deteriorating standards. The downhill slide started in 1964 when private schools were nationalized and English-language teaching in the primary grades was scrapped in favour of the second language being taught only from grade five. The disputable advantage of having been a part of the British Empire, which had given us a head start in the region in the "language of the slave," was now effectively wiped out. Whole generations grew up taught by teachers who had five years of elementary English-language training. State schools, the only ones existing, became crowded, accommodating sixty to eighty students in a classroom. The stick became the only mode of motivation, and the teaching method became that of spoon-feeding and parrot-like learning, if not out of choice, then certainly out of practical exigencies. Teachers were the lowest-paid of government employees, and many resorted to giving private tuition to their own students outside of class, and for an extra charge. What started out perhaps as a necessary evil turned into a stigmatic norm.

The most unfortunate fallout of the 1988 uprising was again in the sphere of education. Historically, the youths of the country and therefore its students had always been at the spearhead for political change. We saw the pivotal roles played by student leaders in the fight for our independence from the British. The students, as aspiring leaders of the future and as the conscience of a new generation, had always taken the initiative for change.

This defining characteristic of the youths and students is anathema to a regime which would not permit any lessening of the tight control they had over the populace. Thus, in order to prevent any such attempts by the students, any sign of such stirrings brought about a general closing down of schools and all educational institutions. They were closed for long stretches without any way of knowing when they would reopen. Also, academic terms were shortened to ludicrous proportions. University education was subordinated to political considerations as campuses were scattered far and wide in out-of-the-way, unheard-of venues. Students and teachers were ferried to underdeveloped satellite towns, where basic amenities were inadequate or non-existent, while the main university stayed empty. Many parents came to see that a serious education for their children, one that would be recognized worldwide and one that would enable them to earn a decent living, had become impossible in their country of domicile.

Our generation of university graduates had successfully carried on the tradition of earlier ones who had taken the opportunity for widening their intellectual horizons by studying abroad in the United Kingdom and the United States in many fields. And they had been able to do that without a hitch in a seamless academic transition after earning their first degree at home. Not so the later ones, except for a few. The young this time were leaving in a small but steady stream for a tertiary education anywhere outside the country, often at great hardship and costs for the family. And more and more, young families in the prime of their working life were looking for employment opportunities abroad "for the sake of their children's education."

Our own family became part of this trend of exodus to lands where the water is clearer and the pasture is greener at least metaphorically!

My sister-in-law Ju Ju was the first to leave her job, at the United Nations Development Programme in Myanmar in 1992, to join the UN's head office in New York City. Moe, who had been retired from the Foreign Service for making his choices clear in the pro-democracy movement of 1988, joined the United Nations Transitional Authority in Cambodia (UNTAC) that same year and went to Cambodia. His son Tin Aung Myaing, who graduated high school from the Practicing School of the Teacher Training College (TTC), went to Bangkok. Very soon afterwards, Pyone and her two sons, Myo and Tun, made plans to move to Bangkok where Htut had preceded them and where Pyone's parents were living in retirement after Uncle U Tun Thein completed his tenure with ESCAP.

Mother was very fragile emotionally after my father passed away. She spoke of going through periods when grief suffocated her. She was not looking for sympathy or solace from us; rather, she was stating a fact. She filled her life with time spent playing cards with friends, going on innumerable grocery shopping trips, knitting or crocheting for her grandchildren, and always looking for an opportunity to treat us to her delightful meals. Every Wednesday morning before dawn she would offer *soon* to the monks on their alms round. If for some reason she was not on time, she would prepare a food container to deliver it at the monastery. Very frequently she would take a specially prepared meal for the monk residing at the zayat of the Bagaya Tawya Monastery, the zayat which was donated by her father,

U Ba San. And once every year on the anniversary of my
father's death, she would hold a *soon kyway,* where five monks
would be invited for a midday meal and where friends and
family asked to join the proceedings, thus enabling her to gain
merit and share it with my father in case he needed it in any
plane of existence he happened to be in.

Kyaw Myaing at Po Chen Tong
Airport in Cambodia while on duty
with UNTAC

In 1992, when plans
were being made for
Mother's two sons and
their families to move
away from the country,
she just listened and
forbore making any
comments. She knew they
had strong reasons for
their decision, and she
realized it was not her call
to make. She suffered
inwardly nonetheless. She who had lived surrounded by
children and grandchildren, and whose special delight was in
gathering all of them together at least on weekends for special
meals, was going to lose half of them to foreign lands and
unknown futures. This time they were not going on government
service in known positions and for predetermined periods. And
she knew it would be difficult for her to visit them. But she kept
her spirits up by planning to attend the graduation of her first
grandson, Aung Thura, in Hawaii in 1993 with her good friend
Daw Kyi Kyi. She asked for and received an invitation from Htut
to visit him in Bangkok, which was the basis for her to apply
for a passport.

At seventy-six, Mother was still very active, enjoying the
company of her many friends, young and old, and planning
special meals for her children and grandchildren. At that time,
her neuralgia was plaguing her. Once she declined going
shopping with me because of a sudden-onset attack. But she
gamely participated in all the farewell lunches and dinners that
were being held by and for the two families who were leaving.
I remember most vividly the dinner at a restaurant to celebrate

my daughter Wai Sann Thi's sixteenth birthday. Mother was at the head of the long table and I was at the other end. For some reason, my brothers had congregated at my end. We were planning something earnestly. I looked up and I saw my mother's gaze on me, a little sad and a little lonely,

My mother and Daw Khin Khin Maw with children and grandchildren

as if she was memorizing my face. Two weeks after that, one early morning in April 1992, she drew her last breath in my arms. She had suffered a fatal heart attack. My two brothers were on the verge of leaving but were in time to attend to her last rites and take care of legal matters. I had to call my son in Maui and tell him the sad news that his *pwa pwa* would not be attending his graduation. His reply was that he would continue to make believe that she was still living while he was away from her presence.

In 1993, Mon Thiri graduated high school from ISY and left for the United States to study at Bryn Mawr College on a scholarship. My youngest brother, Polay, was transferred to the Ministry of Foreign Affairs. Very soon after, in 1994, their family left on a posting to Geneva. At least my mother didn't have to contemplate the departure of the last of her sons, but that left only my husband, me, and our daughter, Wai Sann Thi, in Myanmar. The rest of our extended family now formed part of the huge diaspora that had become a feature of the times.

Tongta, Chie, Phyo Hla Wai, and Wai Sann Thi
at the December 1994 ISY high school graduation

Wai Sann Thi matriculated in March 1992, which made her eligible to enter Yangon University. However, schools and universities had again been closed down for an indefinite period. We figured a beneficial alternative would be for her to join International School Yangon for years eleven and twelve under the American system. This she started in February 1993; she graduated high school in December 1994. By June 1995, the Institute of Economics had reopened, so she attended the first- and second-year courses, passing each year with credit and several distinctions. At this juncture, however, she decided that she wanted to continue her studies in the United States in the same way that her brother and each of her cousins had done. She applied for and was accepted to the Baruch College of the City University of New York for the 1996 academic year.

Chapter 28

The Empty Nest

I retired from my job as business manager at the International School of Yangon in July 1999, six months after I turned sixty, with a service of nearly twelve years. It was the most rewarding experience of my life both professionally, in terms of acquiring efficient work practices and enjoying the greatest work satisfaction, and financially, for ISY teachers and staff were some of the best paid in the country. ISY was the only international school in existence at the time (until about 2001) where children of diplomats and the expatriate business community were educated with an American curriculum. It had grown into a fully accredited international school, offering preschool through grade twelve, with an enrolment topping three hundred at the time I left. Entrance to the school was highly sought after among Myanmar students, who were accepted on a strict quota to maintain the international character of the school.

My granddaughter, Chan Myay, was born to Thi Thi and Aung Thura in November of the same year. I remember that December as being the coldest in Yangon in a long time. That Christmas, Thi Thi, little Chan, and I sat around the living room table opening Christmas presents all by our lonesome. Far away in America, Wai Sann Thi, her cousins Myo and Tun, and her friends were already in Florida preparing to bring in the new century in Disney World. But we did watch the news on satellite TV and saw the new century dawning first in the Pacific Islands. Then slowly, as it travelled across the globe, we saw the fantastic fireworks display at Sydney Harbour, the big drum being struck at Tokyo, the dragons dancing in Hong Kong, the snow-covered Kremlin in Russia, Big Ben striking the hour of midnight in London, and the countdown in Times Square, New York, which, of course, took place when it was already New Year's Day for us in Yangon. Our own new century was brought in with a midnight feast of Chinese hotpot in our living room for the four of us, Aung Thura, Thi Thi, Ko Soe Myint, and me, with the important addition of little Chan Myay.

In February of 2000, I entered a meditation retreat, the first time ever that I had done so, at the Bago Tenth Mile Forest Meditation Centre of the Shwe Taung Gone Panditarama Sasana Yeiktha. This I thought an appropriate watershed in my life to mark the end of my working career and the time before I celebrated my freedom with what I hoped would be a lengthy sojourn to the West. It was a deeply personal and illuminating experience for me, one which I believed would stand me in good stead and guide me the rest of my life.

Since my daughter had left for her undergraduate studies in the United States, I had been able to visit her for only short periods of time, during school holidays, once in 1997 and again in 1998. This time, after severing ties with ISY, I felt free to visit for as long as I wanted or, rather, as long as I was allowed according to US immigration laws, which permitted generally six months with a possible extension for another six.

In January 2004, I celebrated my sixty-fifth birthday in the company of my colleagues at the school where I then worked, having given up retirement one and a half years into it, almost to the day, in December 2001. The more vocal teachers among them had expressed a preference for the celebration to be held at my home rather than at school. I too wanted my birthday celebration to be more than a perfunctory affair, one where I could show my goodwill and friendship towards my teachers. January is always a good time for outdoor entertaining, and so I took the opportunity to set up a well-planned and carefully executed event down to tiny flower vases and candles on each individual round table. The tables and chairs were hired for the evening, and so was the string of coloured lights. The buffet table was carefully laid out with warming pans, over which big oval dishes of the food were kept warm. Glasses were filled with an assortment of drinks which the teachers could help themselves to. And there was music from a CD player brought out into the garden and playing some instrumental oldies. My guests were charmed by the ambience. I could point out to them the cattleya orchid plant that my daughter had arranged to be brought to me as a birthday gift that morning. I could also show them the card sent by my son and my daughter-in-law with the huge childish scrawl of my four-year-old granddaughter proclaiming, "I love you." For of course they all, my son and his family and my daughter, lived apart from my husband and me. The two of us were the prototypical parents inhabiting the empty nest.

I think, however, that the two of us were resigned to the fact that there would be no young and able family members around to make our lives pleasanter, fuller, and/or easier as we grew older, as had been the traditional way, the way my parents' generation had lived. In fact, my husband and I were content with the knowledge that we have given our children the means to make their way in life successfully in this modern world, even if it meant we were separated from them. We had found our equilibrium and had made some sort of niche for ourselves in our own routines and the activities we had each chosen for ourselves. Like a dog circling, nudging, scraping, and pawing the ground before settling down to sleep, we tried out various routines, demarcated our territories, assumed differing responsibilities, and gave and took liberties in our conjoined lives.

One morning during my daily walk, I noticed the big, fat mangoes hanging from the tree in our neighbour's yard. Our trees were just flowering, although a few branches held clusters of young fruit. The jackfruit tree was also heavily laden, in such abundance that the young fruits had to be picked off and given away and even sold as vegetables. The bougainvillea blossoms swung lazily in the morning breeze and the fragrant frangipani flowers dropped loose from their branches. The Indian magpies twittered and sang on the bare branches of the big fig tree, which was just waiting for its refurbishing coat of new foliage. In the quiet of the early morning, songs and chatter of other birds could be identified: the busy chatter of the mynahs, the raucous caw of the crows, and even the echoing cries of the cuckoo, come to announce the arrival of spring.

The days were already growing longer, the sun rising earlier by the day, and I no longer needed a warm jacket to start off my walk. As I walked back and forth on the roadway in front of the house saying my prayers, my eyes lit on the annuals and perennials I had cultivated in flower beds and pots. I could not stay away from the flowers I had known in childhood in my mother's garden, the phlox, the petunias, and the cannas. I also had other flower varieties now, newly popular ones like impatiens and kalanchoe. Big bushes of hibiscus were my husband's specialty. He had them in a whole range of colours, golden yellow, bright orange, scarlet, pale mauve, pale yellow, and pink as well as white. They would choose to bloom, sometimes in turns or several together, so there was a special quality of surprise in seeing which colour was blooming on any particular day. And that would be a subject of comment between us as we said, "Did you notice that beautiful golden yellow blooming today?" or "What a profusion of those scarlets," and so on.

Our children had left the family fold several years ago. Aung Thura's second year at the University of Rangoon coincided with the tumultuous political upheaval of 1988. Schools and universities were closed. I dared not keep him in Yangon, where young students were being hounded in a long trail of suspicion of their involvement in the anti-government uprising. His father, working in Bangkok at that time, and I decided to move our son to continue his studies there. However, Ko Soe Myint was just about to end his stint of working abroad. After settling Aung Thura in a small shared apartment, my husband came home, leaving our son to study and work and struggle on alone.

Aung Thura started again as a freshman at Assumption Business Administration College in Bangkok. After two years there, he transferred to Hawaii Pacific University, from where he graduated. He was having a hard time making ends meet while working and studying since we were not able to support him fully for his tuition and living expenses. Things improved when he was able to work full-time, gaining experience in the hotel industry in Maui. We never fully knew what his long-term plans were: whether he meant to apply for an H1 visa or a green card and stay on and work there, or whether he meant to continue his studies. We had not seen him for about four years when finally fate took a hand and he informed us he would be coming home for a visit. He never returned to Hawaii.

His return in 1995 coincided with the time when Myanmar was embarking on a period of mild economic reforms after abandoning the Burmese Way to Socialism in 1988. The Foreign Investment Law of 1988 was passed, legally allowing foreign private companies to operate. Oil companies like BHP from

Maha Thray Sithu, Lt. Gen. Tin Tun, and Daw Tin Tin Sein bless the couple with jasmine garlands in a traditional ritual

Australia; ARCO and Amoco from the USA; and Total and Premier rolled in. Foreign banks were given licences to open representative offices. Local business entrepreneurs were being encouraged to build hotels in downtown Yangon and seaside resorts. Advertising firms followed in the wake of expanding corporate business. McCann Erickson was one of those international businesses that collaborated with a local partner to introduce new marketing techniques and promotional services for a plethora of consumer products and services that were now being allowed into the country. Aung Thura landed a job with Sail McCann after a two-year stint with one of the first hotels of an international standard to be built and operated by a Myanmar entrepreneur.

He met Thi Thi while working as a manager at the hotel and married her one year later. Aung Thura and Thi Thi were lucky to have the opportunity to be married in the family home of the former's grandparents, the second marriage ceremony to take place at 58 (C) Inya Road just before it was dismantled in 1998. My elder cousin Deputy Prime Minister Lieutenant General Tin Tun, and Daw Tin Tin Sein, had graciously blessed the couple with jasmine garlands in a traditional ritual.

U and Mrs Thaw Kaung, Dr and Mrs Than Aung, and Daw Khin San Yin attend the morning wedding ceremony

Aung Thura and Thi Thi with the groom's father at the evening reception

Aung Thura moved away after his marriage to take on a post with McCann Erikson in Vientiane, Laos. His wife, Thi Thi, stayed behind to give birth to our first grandchild just before the turn of the century in November 1999. And on my first prolonged trip abroad after my retirement from ISY, I took both mother and child to Bangkok and handed them over to my son, who had come from Laos to collect his family.

Wai Sann Thi returned from the United States after working for a year after her graduation from Baruch College, CUNY, in June 2000. She had been on the point of asking her employer to sponsor her for an H1 visa to enable her to stay on and work in New York. Again for Wais, as her friends and cousins called her, fate stepped in. After miles of email conversations and hours of phone calls over a seven-month period, Cameron Russell came from Perth to meet her in New York. During the three weeks of Cameron's visit, the two decided that they wanted a future together. When Ko Soe Myint was told of his daughter's intentions to marry someone who was not Myanmar, he was totally stunned and speechless. I had to make the call from New York, since I was visiting at the time and he was alone in our house in Yangon. He had always maintained that he was quite prepared that his daughter, who had left home to study and work abroad, had the likelihood of meeting and marrying a foreigner. In actual fact, when faced with the reality he could not handle it, or rather he needed time, a longish time, to get used to the idea. Wais first had to visit Perth to meet Cameron's family and to see whether she could be happy there. And Cameron had to come to Yangon to meet Wais' father. When he came, Ko Soe Myint went with Wais to meet him at the airport.

Our daughter spent about six months with us while she waited for a spouse visa to Australia. When that came through, she had to leave immediately to arrive in Perth by a fixed date. I had never dreamed that the time she left for university after her high school graduation from ISY in 1996 would also be the time she left her family for

Wai Sann Thi and Cameron with marriage celebrant and flower girl Sarah Williams

good. She has never come back to live with us since then, only to visit us. Four years is a long time to be parted from my daughter, or so I thought at the time of her leaving with other young friends of hers on her great adventure. If I had known it would be forever, how could I have borne the feeling of desolation?

Wais and Cameron's wedding in March of 2002 was unlike any wedding that we had seen in Yangon. There was none of the pomp and ceremony, none of the crowds, and none of the elaborate jewels and silks on either bride or guests. The

Wedding ceremony at Queen's Park, Perth, 23 March 2002

ceremony was held under a spreading tree on the manicured green lawns of Queens Garden in Perth in the last days of the Australian summer. About thirty family and friends joined the couple for the happy occasion. A marriage celebrant conducted the ceremony, rings were exchanged, and a poem was read in the couple's honour by one of the family friends. Wais' uncle Htut flew in from East Timor and stood in for her father. I was there, of course, having arrived a week earlier to help set up their first apartment in Maylands. I had brought the bridal outfit for Wais, a pale pink beaded top and a layered skirt embroidered with sequined flowers climbing up the hem. There were matching beaded slippers and a bag. Her only ornaments were the ruby necklace and bracelet that were my wedding presents for her, and her ruby and diamond earrings left for her by her grandmother. Friends of ours offered to make the bridal posy of vibrant scarlet gerbera; a coronet for the only flower girl, Sarah, Cameron's niece; and corsages for the bridal party.

The bride and the bride's mother at Maylands before the wedding

Early the next morning, the bride, the groom, my brother, and I made our way to a monastery for a celebratory *mingalar soon kyway,* to receive the blessings of the presiding monk in a traditional Buddhist ceremony. There we were joined by our good friends Dolly and Heinz.

I remember the last night Wais spent with me before I gave her away in marriage.

It was filled with poignancy as we lay facing each other. My thoughts were all of the past, of the times when her love was wholly for her family, when the sun rose and set for her amidst the smiles on our faces. My thoughts shifted and changed like a kaleidoscope, the recalled scenes just as vivid as if the events happened yesterday. I smiled at her with the tenderness of the moment, and she smiled back with the anticipation of the love and happiness that lay ahead for her. We talked a bit. Finally, when we decided we had better get a good night's sleep, she turned over and I lay awake contemplating the swaying hibiscus outside the bedroom window. It had such beautiful pale mauve flowers.

Part III

A Wider World

(2000~08)

Chapter 29

A Wider World

The extended Myaing family, comprised of three generations
of U Tha Myaing and Daw Aye Myaing's descendants, at
U Soe Kyi and Daw Khin Sann Yin's residence on Thaton Road

Apart from the times when we were taking short trips abroad,
my husband and I spent the first decade of the new century
in blissful solitude at 58 (E) Inya Road. We occasionally faced
minor domestic crises and overcame them as best we could.
Polay and Ta Ta were next door at 58 (D) Inya Road. However,
their return from Washington, DC, in early 2005 meant they
had missed the wedding of their elder daughter, Mon Thiri
Myaing, to Jin Yamamoto, which was held in December that
year. It had taken place in Princeton, New Jersey, where Jin's

parents lived. Mon's maternal uncle Khai Mong, as well as his paternal uncle Moe and his wife, Ju Ju, stood in for her parents at the ceremony. She looked radiant in the traditional Myanmar bridal dress that her mother had made and sent to her.

There were visits from my brothers and sister-in-law in New Jersey, my son and family from his postings in Vietnam and later Thailand, and my daughter and son-in-law from Australia, all of which provided little pockets of excitement and an excuse to lay out scrumptious meals. Except for my two children, the rest of the seven grandchildren of my parents were in the United States, either studying or working.

Mon Thiri Myaing marries Jin Yamamoto in 2005. Here with sister Amara at the wedding in Princeton, New Jersey

It seems that the fourth-generation Myaing clan, descendants of my grandparents U Tha Myaing and Daw Aye Myaing (my father's side of family), was now widely spread out around the world, the majority in both the East and West Coast of the USA, but also in Canada, Britain, and Japan – and fairly large contingents in Singapore and Australia – whereas the rest had remained in Myanmar.

Daw Khin Ant, U Tun Sein, and U Kyawt Myaing, the surviving daughter and sons of U Tha Kyawt and Daw Wa Khin, are now all settled in Myanmar. Daw Khin Ant's two daughters, Aye Aye Tun and Tin Tin Tun, were both working abroad when Aye Aye returned to be with her elderly parents. Tin Tin Tun, however, works and lives with her

Cousins and sisters-in-law at a family reunion.

husband and son in Tokyo. U Tun Sein is a well-known artist and a one-time schoolteacher who lives with his surviving son, Zin Moe, and daughter, Moe Moe Thit, in Mandalay. U Kyawt Myaing is a retired flight operations manager of the Union of Burma Airways. He has two daughters practising medicine. Kyawt Kyawt Aye works in Washington State, and Malay Myaing works and lives in San Diego, California, with her husband and two children. The elder son, Aye Kyawt Myaing, works in Canada. The youngest son, Myo Kyawt Myaing, a celebrated pop singer and composer, lives in Yangon. Thus we have U Kyawt Myaing and Daw May May Tin travelling every year to spend part of the time with their daughters and grandchildren in the United States.

U Hla Thwin's surviving daughter, Khin Saw Thwin, has two sons and two daughters working and living in Sydney, Australia, which again meant fairly frequent visits for Saw Saw, or Noreen as she is known to her friends, to see her children and grandchildren. Ko Win Pe, the elder son, had died at age twenty-seven from a congenital heart defect, leaving his wife, Sein Sein Yee, and daughter, Swe Swe Win. One of Swe Swe Win's two sons is now working in Perth, Australia.

Daw Mya Khin's only son, U Ohn Myint, had four children, one of whom is in the United States and another of whom is in Malaysia. The eldest son and youngest daughter still live with their mother in Yangon after U Ohn Myint's demise in 1992. U Ohn Myint had been a district commissioner in Myitkyina at one time. I still treasure the jade cut stones, now fashioned into a necklace, that he gave me as a wedding gift.

The eldest of U Thein Yin's daughters, Khin Nyunt Yin, has one daughter, Thida Win, and two sons, Htin Aung and Win Maw, who all live and work in California. The eldest daughter, Yin Yin Win, who is a doctor, lives and works in the United Kingdom. The second daughter of U Thein Yin, Khin Sann Yin, has two daughters, Saw Nandar Kyi and Muyar Kyi, who live with their families in Singapore. The three other daughters, Thandar Kyi, Ohmar Kyi, and Thuzar Kyi, are all settled in Yangon. The youngest of U Thein Yin's daughters, Khin Thann Yin, is a career woman who retired as deputy director general of the Ministry of Finance and subsequently worked for four years as general manager of the Myanmar Industrial Development Bank. She lives with her two sons in Myanmar, but her eldest daughter, Aye Aye Khine, an eye surgeon, works in Queen Victoria Hospital, East Grinstead, West Sussex, in the United Kingdom. Her youngest daughter, Khin Wai Wai Khine, works and lives in Columbia, Missouri, with her son. Also known to her friends as Elsie, Khin Thann Yin often goes to visit her daughters for months at a stretch.

U Tin Maung's surviving daughter, Than Than Tin (Margaret), and her two daughters, Jade and Jasmine, and son, Justin, live in Canada. U Tin Maung's only son, Tin Aung San (Dicky), lives in the United States. Than Than Nwe (Betty), the eldest daughter, passed away at an early age while working in Cambodia. Betty's eldest daughter, Mya Thida, works in the United States, while another daughter, Khin Sandar, and a son, Min Baw, live in Yangon.

U Twe Maung's eldest son, Than Htut (or Jon), landed in Bristol, England, in the 1970s, got married, and lived there for more than ten years with his wife, Carmen, and son, Duane. Eventually moving to join his wife and son, who had gone ahead earlier to the United States, he has lived there ever since. Three other brothers, Soe Htut, Aung Htut, and Aye Htut, and a sister, Tin Nu Htwe, all live in Yangon. Soe Htut's two daughters, Thet Thet Soe and Thazin Soe, live with their families in Yangon. Tin Nu Htwe's only son, Thet Htwe Aung, works in Singapore.

Consequently we find our generation of parents criss-crossing the globe as we visit the children and each other for months at a time. What started out as fledglings leaving the nest became an introduction to a wider world for their parents' generation.

Another family reunion representing the offspring of
five sons of U Tha Myaing

Chapter 30

New York, New York

The two brothers Htut and Moe with Pyone and Ju Ju at Bear Mountain

The first time I was in New York in 1997 was when I visited my daughter and my brother Moe and his family, with whom Wais lived with in New Jersey. Wai Sann Thi was studying at Baruch College of the City University of New York. The reason she had chosen to study there, aside from the financial reason, was so that she could live with her uncle and aunt while doing so. A typical Asian mother, I could not contemplate my daughter living on her own elsewhere at that tender age. My brother Htut and his family were living in Fort Lee, New Jersey, at the time. And it just made it more of a safety net for my daughter to have another uncle and aunt, and more cousins, living nearby. It meant that one or the other of her cousins, uncles, or aunts could take her out to show her the ropes in a completely strange new environment. But life in New York being such as it is, it was never easy for Wai Sann Thi to get someone to show her the way around more than once. She had to learn to swim or else sink like so many other youngsters before her and since. There were many expensive and teary phone calls that year between mother and daughter, but I had underestimated the young girl's resilience and toughness. Very soon I was getting reports of her visits with her old schoolmates Zar Zar and Thiri and Win Maung to the East Village and many places elsewhere. Pictures came back to me of her going off to see *The Nutcracker Suite* ballet with her aunt as a special treat for her first Christmas in New York, at an Italian

The four cousins Tam, Myo Htut, Tun Htut, and Wai Sann Thi enjoy the snow in New Jersey

restaurant with her uncles and aunts and cousins, in front of the UN building with her cousin Mon, who had come down from Michigan, and with cousins at Rockefeller Center with the Christmas decorations as a backdrop. So when the time came for my husband and I to visit her in June of 1997, she had become a savvy young New Yorker, within the sphere of her little world, that is.

That year, once I had taken earned leave from my job at ISY, my husband and I took the long flight to land at LaGuardia Airport. My sisters-in law Pyone and Ju Ju were as excited about our visit as my brothers were. They all came to meet us. Being in the lap of family anywhere else in the world was home, and we soon forgot we were in a foreign country. This, simply, was our world in a new setting. But what a setting! Ju Ju, who had taken on the role of a cultural guide to the city, had booked us tickets to see *The Phantom of the Opera,* in its ninth year on Broadway. I can think of no other production more likely to impress a first-timer than *The Phantom of the Opera.* I came away starry-eyed and with the music ringing in my ears. Every visit hence to New York had to have a Broadway show as part of the itinerary. Thus, *Beauty and the Beast* and *42nd Street* were added to the jewels of my New York experience. We did not do too many touristy things except when we went to the Metropolitan Museum of Art to see the Hope Diamond. Instead, we would meet for lunch at the UN building or else walk in Bryant Park while we snatched a bite from the pushcarts selling fajitas or Mexican tacos. I had to have an ice cream wherever we went. And I would never settle for a fat-reduced version or a frozen yogurt in place of a Ben and Jerry's or a Häagen-Dazs, which were available only here and not in my country.

Moe, Ju Ju, and Tin Aung Myaing take us out to dinner in Edgewater, New Jersey

I don't think I could have braved the rush hour. I felt sure I would have been lifted along without my feet touching the ground in the stampede of high heels and shoes. But a few hours later, when the older generation came out carefully coiffed and made up, wearing elegant suits and with jaunty kerchiefs tied around their necks – not the least important part of their grooming being the delightful scents that emanated from them – I could sidle into that pace and rhythm. So whenever my husband and I had a date to meet Ju Ju or Wai Sann Thi in the city during lunch hour or after work, we would take the mid-morning buses from New Jersey to cross the Hudson River through the Lincoln Tunnel to disembark at 42nd Street. Then from the Port Authority Bus Terminal, we would either take the New York City Transit buses to go downtown or just walk and walk and walk to wherever we fancied. There were a million things we could see. One time we ended up at the Trump Tower; another, at Macy's. Once we walked to Times Square and gazed and gawked at all the shops along the way. When it was time, we made our way to the appointed place for our meeting. From there it was then a guided trip to Ollie's or to Chinatown for dinner.

In 1997, Pyone was still in relatively good health despite taking treatment for her breast cancer, which had only recently been diagnosed. She had gone first to San Francisco, on her own, leaving my brother and her two sons in Bangkok, where Htut worked in a construction firm and the two sons went to school in Ruam Rudee while living with Pyone's parents in Sukhumvit Road. Later she moved to NYC where Ju Ju, her cousin as well as sister-in-law, was already settled in a UN General Services job. Ju Ju, who had worked for the UNDP in Yangon, had no problems getting a job at the United Nations in New York. In the same way, having worked in the US Embassy in

Moe, Ju Ju, and Tin Aung Myaing with the Twin Towers in the background

Myanmar, Pyone faced little difficulty in getting a job similar to Ju Ju's at the same UN agency. So the two cousins, and the two brothers they married, were quite happily settled in Queens at the time when Wai Sann Thi, their niece, was sent to avail herself of their generous hospitality in the course of her studies in the United States.

I felt undying gratitude whenever I thought about Moe and Ju Ju's immediate invitation for Wais to come and stay with them after I had broached the subject to them in a letter. Pyone extended the same invitation, although her situation at the time was not as strong as Ju Ju's since she had only started to bring her own family over to join her. Very soon after my daughter's arrival, Moe and Ju Ju started to look for a more spacious apartment in New Jersey. Thus it was that when we visited for the first time, we shared Wai Sann Thi's room, which looked out through huge glass windows at the panoramic view of the Bronx across the Hudson. I realized every word was true of New York as "the city that never sleeps." Each time I woke up in the middle of the night, and I woke myself just for that, I looked out and there it was: the New York skyline, blazing and twinkling in a myriad of fairy-tale lights. It was a sight I can never forget.

The first thing about New York City I fell in love with was the *Today* show with Katie Couric and Matt Lauer, and

Al Roker with his weather forecast for the United States and for others' "neck of the woods" wherever it happened to be. There was so much enthusiasm and camaraderie, so much cheer and brightness ready to surface anytime, whatever serious topic they were bringing to the attention of the public or however important a guest they may be interviewing. Always there were serious, meaningful discussions that made me think. If a light note was needed, there was always one sure to bring a smile to your lips. On thinking back, of course, I had never before come across this type of media hype. I was entranced, caught in its spell forever. However many other morning shows I enjoyed later on, this remained my favourite for all time. I went so far as to get up at four o'clock in the mornings while in Perth, Australia, to catch the show. Sure enough, Al's promise of the weather predictions for my neck of the woods included Western Australia.

Then there was the time when tall ships sailed up the Hudson from the Verrazano Bridge to the George Washington Bridge in a celebration called the Festival of Tall Ships. We were ensconced in Ju Ju's apartment at the time. As we had lunch in her cosy dining room, we could gaze at the ships elegantly sailing up the river. Commenting on the different styles of sails and rigging of perhaps half a dozen ships that came into our view, we savoured a moment of rare enjoyment. On the Fourth of July, we enjoyed another spectacle when we took our places with other residents of the apartment block at the top of an embankment to watch the fireworks display across the river.

The most memorable time for me, however, was the year after I retired from my position as business manager at ISY in December 1999 and Ko Soe Myint and I went for a long holiday to visit my

ISY Director David Shawver, Amy, boss, and colleagues visit us in New Jersey

brothers. We attended the thirty-fifth commencement exercises of Baruch College, CUNY, in June 2000, where Wais was one out of perhaps a thousand-plus graduates who were conferred their degrees at Madison Square Garden, the commencement address being given by Harry Belafonte. She had graduated magna cum laude.

Htin Myaing "giving back" to a group of young orphans in Dili, East Timor

That was also the time when we said our farewells to my sister-in-law Pyone, who passed away at age fifty-four, after a five-year-long struggle against cancer. I had spent a few days with her in her apartment, not realizing these were to be almost her last. Htut was with the United Nations Transitional Authority in East Timor (UNTAET), providing engineering services to the UN Peacekeeping Force, and Pyone was alone when her two sons, Myo and Tun, went to school or work. Together we enjoyed watching old movies starring Gregory Peck, Cary Grant, and Audrey Hepburn. We arranged photographs in new albums and talked about going to see some friends in San Francisco. A few days later, Pyone's sisters came to be with her and I went back to Wais' apartment. I heard that Pyone had shared some special moments with her sisters, including a picnic at Bear Mountain. After Wai Sann Thi's graduation ceremony, the three of us dropped in to see Pyone at the hospital. She lay in her hospital bed with her eyes closed while *parittas* were played from a tape recorder beside her. Wais talked to her, and that was the last contact we had with her. Pyone died two days later, on 3 June 2000. The UN section that she worked for conducted a memorial service for her at the interfaith church on 44th street. The service was attended by many of her colleagues and friends while we carried out our own Buddhist rituals at home. When it was time to take care of her ashes, my brother and her two sons decided that Bear Mountain, as a place Pyone had loved, would be an appropriate place to scatter them. I went along to take Pyone's earthly remains to their resting place.

I made my daughter's studio apartment in New Jersey my base for nine whole months. From there, I made forays to the West Coast to visit San Francisco, Los Angeles, and San Jose, thanks to the generous hospitality of my school friends Shirley and Alwin, who not only put me up in their home in San Francisco but also drove me on the coast road to Los Angeles and San Jose. In LA, I met with my cousin Jon and his family, and the children of my cousin Ma Ma Kitty (Khin Nyunt Yin).

My husband and I also went to visit my youngest brother in Paris. From Paris we took the Eurostar for a Channel crossing through the tunnel to London. From London we took the budget airline to Glasgow, and from there took the train for a day trip to Edinburgh. We spent the day sightseeing on a tourist bus, visited Edinburgh Castle, where the famous military tattoo is held every

Htin Myaing with his colleagues at a handing-over ceremony in Dili, East Timor. The Japanese contingent is in the background.

summer, and took pictures like any tourist beside the immobile guard in kilt and sporran. Then I retraced my route to New York, having parted company with Ko Soe Myint, who flew from Paris to visit his good friends Lee and Linda Bigelow in Saint-Jeannet on the Côte d'Azur, before heading back home.

Wai Sann Thi's studio apartment was on the fourth floor of an apartment building among rows and rows of apartment blocks built on an escarpment lining the Hudson River. The more expensive ones faced the river and had a view across it to the west New York skyline. Hers faced the road, and as such I had the convenience of finding the bus stop right in front of the doorstep. Thus, every morning when she went to work I could see her from a window of her apartment as she walked to the bus stop and boarded the NYC Transit bus. Living in one room equipped with a bed, a desk for the computer, a round Burmese lacquer table (on loan from the Htin Myaings), and a TV set was a novelty and a challenge. A tiny kitchenette with a gas stove, a proportionately small refrigerator, and a sink area occupied one end of this room. On one half of the corridor leading from the main door was a small bathtub and shower stall, and a dressing area with a mirror and a built-in wardrobe. It was compact and equipped with all basic necessities. I had one of my happiest times sharing my daughter's life as she worked as an entry-level assistant with a real-estate agent and we cheerfully made do with the bare necessities. Back home in Myanmar, a house with a garden and maids stood half empty as Ko Soe Myint, alone by himself, after his return from Saint-Jeannet, rattled around in it.

This was Wai Sann Thi's first time living in an apartment of her own. She had to pay over $800 in monthly rent, a whopping sum for someone paying out of her own wages from an entry-level job. Previously, she was sharing with three other friends in a three-bedroom apartment in Astoria, Queens, on first leaving her aunt and uncle's apartment in New Jersey. Now I took great pleasure in hanging pictures and ornaments that reminded us of home. I had little pots of African violets, and a frail-looking jasmine plant which I coaxed to flower by keeping it warm on the radiator while the window nearby let in the morning sun. And I cooked Myanmar food every day!

I slid easily into a satisfying routine of prayers, breakfast, watching the morning show, and walking to the corner grocery store in the mornings. I had a light lunch of noodle soup with lots of fresh vegetables and cooked meat as I watched the soaps: *Days of Our Lives* and *The Bold and the Beautiful,* to mention a few. Then, while I tidied and cleaned or prepared dinner, I watched *Oprah, Judge Judy,* and *Men Are from Mars.* Sometimes I spent long hours on the Internet, tying up the phone line which worried my daughter, who couldn't check on me during her lunch break. During this time, I had the luxury of being free for entire days to watch the events of the 2000

Olympics, held in Sydney. I followed my favourite team, Katie and Matt, as they covered the events at Bondi Beach. I had my first glimpse into American politics as election fever rose to a pitch that autumn of 2000. I watched with avid interest and an almost obsessive fascination as the tide of victory turned for Al Gore and then for George W. Bush, until it became almost farcical with the counting and recounting of the votes in a small, hitherto inconsequential state. All of the vote counters turned into stars as national TV zoomed in on their serious faces.

In that amazing year, one crowded with new sights, sounds, and sensations, I enjoyed a gem of an experience when my brother Moe and his wife, Ju Ju, took me to Vermont to see the changing colours of the autumn landscape. All along the route, we could see ahead wave after wave of every imaginable autumn hue as the forests' leaves imperceptibly change colour. The air was crisp and invigorating when we stopped for a roadside fair, festive with its stalls of baubles and beads, home-made crafts, and everything to excite your curiosity; or when we stopped at an isolated farm offering an irresistible chance to pluck your own fruits off the tree. At the small chalet where we stayed, we donned woollen caps and took leisurely strolls in the evening as we enjoyed the crisp autumn air. The next morning we walked into the city centre and explored as many small shops as we could take in, overstimulated as we were with the plethora of goods on display. We took pictures beside piles of golden pumpkins of every size and intruded on straw figures of the scarecrow standing and sitting on benches with other characters from *The Wizard of Oz.*

That same year, Moe drove us down to Washington, DC, where we were put up at the house of Ko Soe Thin, Moe's one-time colleague from MOFA, and his wife. We were happy to meet up with our friend Helen, who was then head of the Asian Division of the Library of Congress. Helen as well as her mother, Aunty Daw Mya Sein, had become very good friends with Ko Soe Myint since his young diplomat days in Washington, DC, from 1961 to 1966. Also, as it happened, Helen's brother Ko Mya Baw had met my cousin Betty in New

York during this time and married her one year later in Yangon. Betty was the eldest daughter of my uncle U Tin Maung who was then deputy permanent representative to the United Nations under U Thant.

My old friends Ko Tun Aung and Jenny, hearing of our visit, invited us to a meal at their house. I was thrilled to see my college mates Maureen and Daphne Hla Kyi, whom I hadn't seen for almost forty years. Khin Soe Win, or Ma Lon, who had been a colleague of my brother Moe at the Foreign Office, had then settled in Washington, DC, and was working at the Voice of America. She invited us for *mohinga*, which is our all-time favourite dish, never refused at any time of the day. We had a grand old time catching up.

Aunty Sally, Maureen, and Daphne Hla Kyi join us, Ko Soe Thinn, and Moe at a lunch hosted by Ko Tun Aung and Jenny

School friends Sherlie and Alwyn drive me down
the coast road to Los Angeles and San Jose

Win Maw, Jon, me, Duane, and Cici in Los Angeles

Chapter 31

Paris and London Revisited

H. E. U Linn Myaing with French
President Jacques Chirac after
presentation of credentials

While in the United States, my husband and I had applied for a Shengen visa and flown to Paris, where my youngest brother, Linn Myaing, was Myanmar's ambassador to the French Republic and was also ambassador, permanent delegate, to UNESCO. He had presented his credentials to President Jacques Chirac in 1999. He was also appointed ambassador to the kingdoms of the Netherlands and Belgium and to the Swiss Confederation with residence in Paris in 2000.

Po lay and Ta Ta gave me a huge room to sleep in. It was full of elegantly old furniture and looked down onto a garden dominated by a beautiful big tree. I used to love lying on the bed in the afternoons and listening to the French news on the radio to get a feel for the sound of the spoken language while gazing at the swaying branches outside. Incredibly, the residence was the same 60 rue Ampere, although, of course, I could not remember it at all from the first visit. It was five storeys high, which meant that I had to climb up to the breakfast room connected to the kitchen for every meal. The formal dining room was one floor higher still, from where I could see the iron doors of the dumb waiter in a corner. I requested croissants or brochettes for every breakfast. Mar Thee and Ahmee, the two maids who had accompanied my hosts, enjoyed taking me to the nearest farmers' market for fresh fruits and vegetables. We walked past some grand old homes and tennis courts and along quiet lanes until we reached the market identifiable by gaily coloured umbrellas and carts and stalls manned by sellers of various nationalities.

Ta Ta takes me on an enchanting tour of the Palace of Versailles

This time I was in Paris for a month, and I had ample time and facilities, provided by my brother and sister-in-law, to make up for a lot of things I had missed the first time around. They took me for walks down the Champs-Élysées. In the company of our ISY friends, we enjoyed a boat ride down the Seine, past the lovely spires of Notre Dame Cathedral situated on the Île de la Cité. I read up on the royal romance between Napoleon and Josephine before going on a tour of Empress Josephine's chateau. Ta Ta enthusiastically took me to the many lovely gardens around Paris' arrondissements, and once on a long walk to the Tuileries, not really realizing how great the distance was. Polay and Ta Ta, each in turn, took me for almost daily walks to the nearby Parc Monceau with its huge trees and large expanses of rolling green lawns. Some trees had uprooted during a recent storm. I marvelled at the sheer size of the trunks; they made me think of how long they had once stood in glorious splendour. The visit to the Palace of Versailles, the walk in the Hall of Mirrors, and the march down the terraced steps of the garden where water fountains played to the music of Mozart were certainly unforgettable. Equally unforgettable was the visit to Monet's garden to see the profusion of flowers of the special colour palette favoured by Monet and the poppies and the water lilies that had inspired his famous paintings. One month quickly passed with many trips to Sephora on the

Champs-Élysées, where I never tired of trying out the heady perfumes. I finally bought a few.

Ko Soe Myint and I with Linn Myaing and Thi Thi Ta at their Paris residence

From Paris we took the Eurostar for a Channel crossing through the tunnel to London, where our friends Dr Kyaw Win, the Myanmar ambassador, and his wife, Daw Kyi Kyi, provided us with warm hospitality for two weeks. They took us to the Buddhist monastery of Reverend Thila Nanda Bivhamsa, walked us to the grounds of the beautiful mansion where the movie *Notting Hill* was filmed, drove us to Brighton on a fine summer's day, and indulged me with a nostalgic visit to LSE and what used to be my digs at No. 8 Onslow Gardens. They also took us to see the Cirque du Soleil at the Millennium Dome. When we were not out being shown around by my friend Kyi Kyi, we enjoyed the company of Aye Sandar, her lovely daughter, who took us out for walks around the neighbourhood with her toddler Than Thar in a stroller.

Ko Soe Myint with Dr Kyaw Win and Daw Kyi Kyi

Kyi Kyi and I stop for a picture in front of Trafalgar Square

Ko Sonny (Dr Maung Maung Lwin) was remarried by this time to Wai Wai (Dr N. Wai Khine), and she kindly took me out to watch *The King and I* at the London Palladium. Afterwards the three of us enjoyed dinner at an Indian restaurant. I was happy to see Ko Sonny again after so many years, since the time when I was in London as a student and he and my cousin Lily had been such pillars of support for me. They had been classmates at medical school in Yangon and, shortly after completing their studies, had married and moved to London. She had been a brilliant eye surgeon. Sadly, she died of cancer in her prime.

Chapter 32

Scotland

Lately, I had begun to express my views on travelling by saying that I visited places primarily to be with friends or family and not just to see the wide, wide world, as marvellous and fascinating as I knew it could be. I make that distinction because I remember in my young days that my passion was to see places, to imbibe the glamour of a place like Venice or Verona or the Côte d'Azur.

I travelled this time to Glasgow to be with my cousin Timothy Khin Saw (the second son of my maternal aunt Cissy) and his charming wife, Pyone, who visited us often in Yangon when they were there. Their invitation to visit them was warm and genuine enough for me and my husband not to feel we would be imposing on them. They are a busy couple, both medical practitioners, but my cousin had offered to time his vacation so that he would be free to take us around during our visit.

The low-fare plane trip from London was a product of the times. It involved buying seats online and just showing up at the airport with proof of identity, at which point you were given a boarding pass for the appropriately named EasyJet, a Boeing 737. This being a no-frills trip, seats were not assigned and, understandably enough, no meals were served. A trolley came by with drinks and small eats that you could pay for. The journey took fifty-five minutes in all from Luton Airport near London to Glasgow International. And it was obvious that the travellers were mostly business people commuting between the two cities.

When we got off, we found that it was a perfect summer day, bright blue skies and warm sunshine. From the city, we crossed the River Clyde and my cousin pointed out to me the great Clyde shipyards where ocean liners such as the *Queen Elizabeth* were built. For some reason, Glasgow had ceased to be the highly industrial city that it used to be before; as a result, the city had become cleaner. We drove along part of the highway which seemed to me so different from the highways out of New York City, which were very intimidating with their confusing array of signboards and with automobiles whizzing past you at high speed. Here the highways were mostly three lanes. We drove past fields with grazing cattle or sheep, and the vista was all green in the summer. Sometimes in the distance we saw small villages behind clumps of trees. There was a distinct odour in the air, which originated from the heavily manured fields. According to my cousin, this was quite typical of the countryside. However, it was not an unnatural smell. And in the wide-open spaces with so much fresh air around, it was not so off-putting.

As we got into the suburbs, we noticed that the houses we passed by were full of character and very picturesque. Some seemed quite small by our standards, but this was understandable, since they had been built to conserve heat in climatic conditions quite different from ours. These small houses featured little gardens that were filled with plants and flowers carefully planned as to their colour composition, height, and texture. Such a garden was the one that belonged to our hosts, although theirs was rather bigger and terraced, and even boasted a little water pool and fountain. I could not resist putting the pretty scene on record immediately on our arrival. Timothy and Pyone's two large cats with fluffy long coats, obviously much indulged judging by their size, lazily drifted in and out of the scene.

We started the sightseeing immediately that afternoon since we had only three days. Britain is studded with monuments which are declared National Heritage Sites, and the cottage at

Alloway in Ayreshire, belonging to the family of Robert Burns (1759–1796), Scotland's poet, is one of them. If you have ever recited the line "Oh, my love is like a red, red rose" or sung "Auld Lang Syne," then you will know of whom we are talking about. The cottage with its thatched roof protected by wire mesh was preserved to appear basically the same as it had when the family who once lived there had used it. Modern technology, by way of an audiovisual show inside the cottage, aided to inform the visitors of the way the family had lived there, with the one bed shared by all the family, and the kitchen shared by their cattle and hens. "Son of a farmer and a farmer himself," Robert's father had taught him to read and write at the little table displayed by the bedroom window.

Close by in a sort of a triangular arrangement are all the other monuments dedicated to the poet, such as the Tam O'Shanter Experience, which depicts the story told by the poet in his epic poem of that name. We saw the little bridge over which Tam O'Shanter had escaped with his mare, and the ruined church where he had spied the witches' dance. After a whole afternoon was spent strolling around the site amidst gardens adorned with rose bushes and alabaster statues, we returned to the house and enjoyed the rest of the long summer's evening, which lasted until about ten. Our hosts had invited my (and their) young niece and her mother to join us for the evening meal. So it was in the company of family that we closed the first day of our stay in Glasgow.

The next day we took a day trip by coach to visit Edinburgh.

A fine summer day in the lovely garden belonging to
Timothy and Pyone; Glasgow, 2000

Chapter 33

Washington, DC

Ambassador Linn Myaing and Daw Thi Thi Ta with
US President George W. Bush and First Lady Laura Bush

In 2003, we again visited Washington, DC, but this time to savour the warm and thoughtful hospitality that the Linn Myaings – Polay and Ta Ta – always extended for their siblings wherever the former happened to be. My brother had presented his credentials as Myanmar ambassador to the United States of America to President George Bush in June 2001 after having served a two-year term as envoy to Paris, France.

The highlights of our US trip this time were the visit to Gettysburg National Military Park and to the University of South Carolina, where Amara, the younger daughter of Polay and Ta Ta, was studying. Polay, coming from a military background, still showed great interest in such matters and went to great lengths to explain to me strategic elements of the battles between the

At the Gettysburg National Military Park overlooking the Valley of Death

Confederate and the Union armies in the Battle of Gettysburg. He pointed out famous landmarks such as the Devil's Den and the site at which President Abraham Lincoln was supposed to have given the Gettysburg Address. He no doubt was thinking that I shared the same interest with the same intensity, as after-dinner video shows of *The Blue and The Grey* and *Gettysburg* interspersed with our nightly conversations.

Amara's graduation from the University of South Carolina

Since Washington was Ko Soe Myint's first posting as a junior diplomat, he took the opportunity to revisit the chancery buildings, trying to locate his old offices and seeking out local staff with whom he might have worked. Polay, eager to share his favourite personal experience with his new posting, walked us along the route he took to come home, down the Spanish Steps from S Street, every evening after his duties at the embassy were over. The Spanish Steps were constructed as part of the City Beautiful movement in Washington in 1911. We took great pleasure in the walk down the beautiful wide concrete steps shaded by and lined with magnolias, red cedars, and other flowering trees. Two flights of steps curve around a lion-head fountain from a wide terrace to the level below. For Ta Ta, her great challenge in this posting as the ambassador's wife was in entertaining the big Myanmar delegations that arrived in NYC for each UNGA session and took weekend trips to the nation's capital.

While in Washington, I was particularly happy to be able to catch up with Ma Ma Ivy, whom I had known and long admired as the very good friend of my older cousin Lily when they were medical students together in Yangon. Her husband, Ko Jimmy, was the owner of Taw Ein on Inya Road, in which Ko Soe Myint and I had the great good fortune to dwell as our very first home after our marriage.

Moe and Ju Ju drove down from New York to join us for one weekend. We took that opportunity to visit Longwood Gardens, owned by the Du Pont family foundation, in Pennsylvania. It was huge. We could only take in a few conservatories housing orchids and water lilies. We were surprised to find a popular pink climber found in our country, the Rangoon climber. Musical and theatrical performances, dining events, tours, and workshops were advertised for the summer, but there was sadly no time for us to join in any of the activities.

Back at the residence, we rested and looked forward to a scrumptious, authentic Myanmar meal concocted almost magically by Mar Thi and Ah Mee, the two maids who had accompanied the Linn Myaings on their Foreign Service tours to Geneva, Paris, and Washington. Thus we bonded in the most basic and favourite activity of the Myaing siblings and families in a home away from home.

Ta Ta, Ju Ju, and me at Longwood Gardens,
Kennett Square, Pennsylvania

Chapter 34

New Beginnings - Australia

Wai Sann Thi at the spring festival at King's Park, Perth

My visits to Perth, where my daughter now lives with her husband, had a special character about them. My daughter and son-in-law were both embroiled in their jobs and continuing studies. There would be overtime work, which they would invariably take on because they needed the money. There would also be school group projects for my daughter when graduate students like her, who were working family men and women, juggled their work and family routines to make room for academic activities. I was content to fit in with Wai Sann Thi and Cameron's agenda, to shop for groceries and household items they needed for their new house. I would cook for them all the foods my daughter loved and missed, either because she didn't know how to prepare them or because she didn't have the time for the complicated preparation. Cameron never complained about the food I cooked; he liked the curries and would accept most of the dishes that were special to the Myanmar palate. In fact, he had very bravely promised to eat whatever my daughter ate. They attended together the functions put on by the Myanmar community in Perth for special occasions like Thingyan and

Wisak. It made me happy, moreover, that my daughter was able to hold a special *ein tek,* or house-warming, when a couple of Buddhist monks presided, blessed the house and its occupants, and shared merit with every living being. Family friends were present on the occasion; they had brought, in the spirit of *dhana,* special dishes to offer to the monks and, after the monks ate, to share with all those present. Myanmar Buddhist *ahlus* were thus always overflowing with food and sweetmeats, and it was not unusual for unexpected guests to be welcomed into the proceedings and be fed as well.

In the second year of Wai Sann Thi and Cameron's marriage, they were able to afford to buy a small bungalow in a part of Perth close to Cameron's parents, and in a neighbourhood, which they made clear to me was definitely not top drawer. But it was a safe and quiet one nevertheless. There was a bus stop and a

Wai Sann Thi and Cameron on their way to celebrate their second wedding anniversary

railway station close by, considerations important for my daughter, who had not yet the opportunity to drive her own car. Very often Cameron would get up early in spite of having gotten home late, at two or five in the morning, after working overtime all night, and drive Wais to work. Or, he would pick her up from work in the early afternoon and send her to the University of Western Australia, where she did a course or two each trimester towards her MBA. While I was visiting, this was the opportunity I took to shop in the city. I went to the Vietnamese store for Asian groceries.

I enjoyed the quiet and the peacefulness of the spread-out neighbourhoods in Perth. True, it took some driving to visit friends and relatives who lived in various suburbs, north and south of the Swan River, but the roads were a dream to drive on and traffic was light and well regulated. In fine weather, the skies were a deep blue. The fluffy white clouds just added to the picture-perfect scenery. With the absence of high-rises except in the central business district (CBD), one may enjoy a 180° view of the skies overhead. Wai Sann Thi and Cameron made it a point to take my husband and me out on weekends to the many picnic places, such as the Wollongong Dam and Tomato Lake, and to other interesting places, out of which Subiaco Station Street Markets and Fremantle Markets have stayed in my memory.

New friends I made at the local Buddhist monastery and others spread around the city were cordial and accepted me warmly into the community. These new friends and old took me to delightful restaurants, and to beautiful parks and gardens that abound in Perth. The picnics at King's Park, when friends

Friends in Perth gather for a Myanmar meal at Wai Sann Thi's house

brought their special foods to share and we all sat around, talked, and enjoyed the fine weather, made wonderful memories for us all.

In 2003 we flew to Sydney, where we had to attend the wedding ceremony of Ko Soe Myint's nephew, the son of his cousin Noreen and Ko Myo Win. The trip from Washington, DC, to Sydney, Australia, was a marathon flight involving twenty-six hours of flying time and spreading over two days across the International Date Line. We spent a week with our hosts, Tin Aung Win (another cousin) and Dorothy. They took us for lunch along the waterfront in the shadow of the Sydney Harbour Bridge and drove us to the Blue Mountains, there to enjoy the scenery and see famous landmarks like the Three Sisters. The wedding was held in Canberra, and we all drove down for the ceremony and reception. It was an occasion to reunite with Ko Soe Myint's cousins and nieces and nephews, some of whom he had not seen for nearly twenty years. The day after the wedding we took the cross-country flight from Sydney to Perth.

For our visit to Perth this time, our daughter and son-in-law had planned a trip down south to Nornalup. We crossed luxuriant pastureland over rolling hills, passed through giant trees that were hundreds of years old, and saw herds of cattle – brown, black, and heifers – as well as flocks of woolly sheep, all content in great open spaces. Wild flowers blazed along the trail – brilliant yellows and dramatic lilacs. And all along the route was a chance to drop by at a sandy beach since we were skirting the coastline of the mighty Indian Ocean. We dropped by for lunch at just such a place, sat in the car since it was quite windy, and watched a group of surfers trying to ride the waves.

Our hosts had booked the four of us into a chalet at the Nornalup Riverside Chalets. Across the road from us was the Franklin River, little more than a stream at this point. But still the sight of rippling waters in the sunlight was a sight we didn't come by often as the first to greet our eyes in the morning. The chalet had two bedrooms and a pot-bellied wood fireplace in the living area, with a kitchenette complete with all the equipment for cooking, right down to cutlery and china. The bathroom was a marvel of efficiency; it could even accommodate a disabled person in a wheelchair. As the days and nights were a cold, 14°C in the Australian spring, we appreciated the heated rails for our towels and the electric mattresses at night.

As soon as we had settled into our chalet, we started the wood fire, which at first seemed it would be difficult. But everything had been set up in the fireplace, so all we had to do was strike a match. Then I took a cup of steaming-hot coffee and braved the cold outside on an invitingly rustic bench. The lavender and other wild flowers growing in a bed in front of me were fragrant as I breathed in the cool, fresh air. I heard the squawking of birds in a nearby tree. Then one flew right past my line of vision. I didn't pay much attention as I was lost in the peacefulness of the moment. Then I caught the flash of a brilliant green and realized the birds were parakeets. They were as abundant here as crows and sparrows were in my country. I noticed bird feeders hanging from the eaves of our chalet and others nearby. The birds flew in, in twos and threes, to line up at the feeder. I was entranced. I know we have parrots and parakeets in our forests, but none so accessible that I could enjoy the sight of them with a cup of coffee in my hand and a book to read close by.

The bustle of the city was indeed left far, far behind. Everything was very quiet except for the sound of birds. The squawking and the occasional harsh cry of the kookaburra aside, if you listened deeper you could hear the chirping, the trilling, and the various bird cries of innumerable species as if in layers of sound. They were of all sizes, and, except for the big, black crows, all of them were of brilliant hues, the deep vermilion blue and the deep red and green of a church mosaic. I am at a loss for words to describe them. I regretted not having the knowledge or foresight to bring a pair of binoculars. We made up for it by visiting the Walpole–Nornalup National Park to see the beautiful birds, the most remarkable among them being the purple-crowned lorikeet.

On our last morning, when the sun shone bright and white clouds scudded across a blue sky, my husband and I walked over to the river's edge, where a lone fisherman was holding a line. In the marshes on the riverside, tiny birds hunted for food. I couldn't resist taking a picture near the stark outline of a grass tree, a small tree with bare blackened trunks and grass-like leaves sticking out at the top like a mop of unruly hair. As I sat writing this on the trestle bench, enjoying the sights and sounds, a duck waddled underfoot, perhaps searching for crumbs.

My husband and I have made many trips to Perth since then, at least twice a year, when we caught up with friends and joined in various community events celebrating traditional, cultural, and religious occasions both Myanmar and Australian. There were the Thingyan water festivals held at the monasteries, where seasonal foods were served in abundance and where guests performed exuberant songs and dances. We helped at meditation retreats conducted by prominent monks from Myanmar who had come specifically for the purpose by invitation. On a warm summer's evening, we joined a Christmas

Carols by Candlelight event on the community green. We were part of the throngs of people who walked to the foreshore of South Perth to watch a spectacular show of fireworks for Australia Day. The fact that I was not deprived of my Myanmar traditional activities while I was away from my own country endeared my daughter's adopted country to me. Above all, I appreciated getting to know the life that my daughter now lived as a professional career woman with a circle of colleagues and friends and a tranquil home life with Cameron. Her home life could not but be different from the environment she had known with me and her father. I enjoyed being part of it, even if for short interludes.

Chapter 35

Our Neighbours from South East Asia

I was in Vientiane to celebrate my granddaughter Chan's first birthday

Ko Soe Myint and I were lucky to have the opportunity to visit Laos and Vietnam during the time when our son, Aung Thura, was working as an advertising executive with McCann Erikson. These are neighbouring countries which had always fascinated us but which normally slipped out of our travel itinerary because no friend or family were living there. As it was, the lure of seeing our first grandchild and of visiting another country in South East Asia was big enough for us to take multiple trips to Vientiane and Ho Chi Minh City in turn.

Aung Thura's house in Vientiane was double-storeyed and had a big yard. It was similar to houses occupied by expatriates in our own country, complete with a security guard at night. Coming back from a couple of months in New York, where only city sounds dominated, we realized that the cock's crow at dawn and the barking of dogs made us feel that we were very nearly home. Thi Thi took me shopping at the local market where fish abounded and small shops sold noodles and fish baked whole in their skins. We went one day to a small French bakery to order a birthday cake for Chan's first birthday, and I was delighted to find the brochettes similar to the ones in Paris. I was also taken to a silk-weaving centre, where I saw silk skeins being treated with natural dyes in huge vats and then hung out to dry. My most treasured memory of Vientiane is the time Thi Thi, with Chan in her arms, took me to the banks of the Mekong, the river that flows through both our countries, so we could gaze across at the bank opposite to a place I could call my own. There we found a shop among many stretched right along the banks selling delicious baked fish.

Thi Thi with her daughter, Chan, at a beach near Ho Chi Minh City

I found Ho Chi Minh, or Saigon, as it used to be called, to be a more aggressive city. The sounds were louder, and the car horns intruded more. The hundreds of motorcycles rushing at me seemed a terrifying gauntlet to face when crossing the wide boulevards on foot. Street hawkers called out their wares of vegetables or food in the street where my son and family lived. Taxis abounded; one would arrive within five minutes of a phone call and take a person wherever he or she wanted to go. The maid arrived on her own motorcycle, with a cell phone conveniently tucked into the back of her jeans. This fact was remarkable to me since mobile phones were accessible to so few in my own country at that time.

Every morning I was there, Thi Thi walked out to a corner shop to get me a bowlful of *Pher,* a noodle soup with strips of beef served with bean sprouts and fragrant herbs, and accompanied by a sauce and lethal sliced yellow chilli. It was delicious. Anytime I was in a Vietnamese shop in another country, I could never find something that equalled the taste of this simple dish. There was very little oil in the foods the Vietnamese eat, and I felt that accounted for the incredibly slim waists of the girls in graceful *ao dai* as they whizzed past on the backs of their boyfriends' motorcycles.

My son took me to visit the Paradise Golf Club and Beach Resort at Song Pe, a three-and-a-half-hour drive from central Ho Chi Minh City. We saw plantations of dragon fruit. Once, when we stopped at a small beach, we found many fishing boats that were shaped like huge bowls. None of us played golf, but little Chan enjoyed swimming in the pool and walking about the huge compound. Our hosts, Ko Kyi Min and Khin Htwe Kyi, took us to a ceramics factory nearby, where we bought a few irresistible pieces as souvenirs.

Aung Thura was transferred to Bangkok, Thailand, in 2005. He was getting a lot of experience, and he welcomed this move as an opportunity to round off his exposure to the region. I was just happy that my son and his family were being brought closer home to us. It turned out to be an opportune time, because Thi Thi needed to be back home in Yangon to give birth to their second child, a son. Nay Thurein Aung was born in the newly

Ko Soe Myint with his two grandchildren at a beach house in Pattaya belonging to a friend

opened Pun Hlaing International Hospital in September 2005. Back in Bangkok, Aung Thura started looking for an appropriate apartment and a suitable school for little Chan, who had started grade school. Thi Thi, her newborn son, and little Chan were taken back to Bangkok about four months after Nay Thurein's birth

In all my travels to the United States or Australia, or even to the two South East Asian countries I mentioned above, I had never stopped in to visit Bangkok even though it was the hub from which I changed flights to these countries. That was partly because I was travelling alone and I didn't feel up to going into the city on my own. But now that I had my son and family living there and I had a convenient place to lodge, I had no hesitation in spending a weekend or several weeks with them. Naturally, the enjoyment of exploring the city from the comfort of my son's home proved to be an experience superior to doing the same from hotel rooms. I learned to love walking around the neighbourhood markets for fresh fruits and vegetables with Thi Thi and little Nay Thurein in a stroller. Browsing in the night markets was a special delight. On Saturdays, we all went out for massive shopping at Big C and Gourmet Market at the Emporium for a week's supply of groceries. Aung Thura would show off his cooking skills that night with a special dinner featuring what for me was huge amounts of meat in something like an Italian dish called the bollito misto. One weekend, he took us to a floating market; I was like a child at a toyshop salivating at the sight of a mind-boggling variety of spicy foods. And I discovered that street food in Bangkok had become my firm favourite.

I enjoyed having time to spend with my grandchildren, taking little Nay for walks up on the rooftop in the cool of the evenings. Little Chan was already an avid reader. There were already more than a couple of volumes of *Harry Potter* which she had finished on her bookshelf. She also liked drawing very sharp images of girls in fashionable clothes and with modern looks, not at all like the ones I drew, which were sweet, dull, and unoriginal. Having started school at the British International School on Rasimi Road, Chan had to get up before daybreak to take the school ferry. Nay Thurein, at two and a half, was attending a half-day nursery school located in Central World. Aung Thura would walk him there on his way to work. During my visits, Thi Thi and I would drop Nay off at school in the mornings and continue on to whichever department store we had chosen to shop at, picking him up on the return trip. It was indeed a relaxed way to enjoy Bangkok, a city with myriad attractions, but by only a few of which I was content to be diverted.

Aung Thura enjoys time with Nay Thurein at the beach

In 2008, Thi Thi decided to follow her ambition to be a pastry chef. She attended Le Cordon Bleu Dusit Culinary School at Silom. It was a good opportunity to take advantage of their stay in Bangkok and to attend such a well-known institution, but she had a tough struggle on her hands. My son, Aung Thura, was supportive. The two of them together managed to take care of the two children and saw to it that the latters' school and home routines were not neglected. She will finish in 2009 with a *diplome de patisserie*.

Chapter 36

Full Circle

In the cool, dry seasons of January 2007 and 2008, our Myaing family had what we billed to be family reunions, fairly big ones, or the biggest we could get, considering that we lived spread out on three continents and in six cities of the world.

In 2007, I and my three siblings were all together, temporarily, for the first time in years at our family homes in Yangon. Moe and Ju Ju had come accompanied by their son, Tin Aung Myaing, and Jennifer. I had my son, Aung Thura, his wife, Thi Thi, and their two kids; and my daughter, Wai Sann Thi, and her husband, Cameron, all visiting at the same time. Htut's sons couldn't come. Neither could Polay and Ta Ta's daughters. For the two weeks that we could all be together, our schedules were tight, as we had planned a *soon kyway* in memory of our parents, river cruises, dinners out, a traditional *htamane pwe,* and a trip to Ngwe Saung beach on the Andaman Sea.

My family's official 2007 reunion picture

In 2008, it was the turn of Polay's girls, Mon (and her husband, Jin) and Amara, to visit. My son, Aung Thura, and Thi Thi, Chan, and Nay Thurein made up my party. Wais and Cameron were not able to come. Neither could Tin Aung Myaing and Jennifer. Moe and Ju Ju made a later trip. In consideration for the two girls who had not been back home for more than ten years, we all decided to pay a visit to Taunggyi, which was Ta Ta's family home, and the Inlay area. We would take in Kalaw as well. We had a gift exchange in the hotel room of the Aye Thar Yar Golf Resort, where automated toys from the States delighted the two young children, and the exotic silks from Bangkok thrilled the two "American" girls. The boat trip through the Inlay Lake in the early morning mist with the spray whipping our faces, and with the quiet disturbed only by the chug-chugging of the motor boats, with visibility narrowed down to two feet ahead of each boat, was a never-to-be-forgotten experience.

One night as Chan, who was then eight, and I lay in bed in a chalet in Kalaw, she asked me, "How many more years will you live, Pwa Pwa?" We were staying at this hotel in Kalaw built high at the top of a gorge. In the evenings, if we went out to the View Point, we could see the smoke curling up from tiny houses in the valley, for the nights were cold. Rose bushes adorned the garden path that led to the front of each chalet. We had a fireplace in our front room. I was not surprised or shocked by such a question, as Chan had asked me once before quite recently, "When will you die, Pwa Pwa?" I answered, as on that previous occasion, that

My two grandchildren with me at the View Point, at Kalaw Hilltop Hotel, 2008

these are things that we cannot foretell. She persisted, "How long, do you think?" I said then, not wishing to sadden her with the possibility of an abrupt end, that I would die maybe in about ten years, maybe more.

"Do you think it could be about twenty?"

"Maybe. Why?"

"I want you to live until I am about my mommy's age now."

I decided to joke a little in order to lighten the serious undertones of this discussion. "But, Chan, I would be so old by that time I would not be able to do anything fun with you," I replied, alluding to the times we had played hide-and-seek or had staged pillow fights.

"We could still talk" was her answer. And I could find nothing more to say.

My son, Aung Thura, and daughter, Wai Sann Thi, with me on the cruise down the Rangoon River, 2007

Having had the last word, she fell asleep, but I lay pondering and then came to a sudden realization that the heretofore hidden purpose of my writing was, to me, now revealed.

I realize now that, for me, I have been writing my memoir so that I could talk to my grandchildren and my great-great-grandchildren long after I am gone and the possibility of having fun times with them is no more.

My granddaughter, Chan, at age eight with me
at Kalaw Hill Top Hotel, 2008

Afterword

In 2010 Myanmar elected a civilian government into power after almost fifty years of a military dictatorship in one guise or another. No matter that the civilian government that came into power would have a president who was ex-army; that the party that won was the Union Solidarity and Development Party (USDP), an incarnation (with a change in membership) of the Union Solidarity and Development Association (USDA), which was formed by SLORC in 1993; and that 25 per cent of the parliamentary members would be constitutionally appointed military personnel. From any viewpoint, this situation left a great deal to be desired. But that was the extent of the reforms that we could practically hope for at that time; it was either take it, or leave it at the status quo. At that stage, none of the contenders inside the political arena or outside of it wanted that. Everyone knew a change had to be made or else – and a peaceful transition was all most of us wanted and were thankful for. We all knew a lot lay ahead.

A political system defines the kind of life its citizens live under. The coup d'état that brought socialist military rule to the country in 1962 was felt like a violent shock to the lives of those who had grown up under parliamentary democracy. Everyday living was hard; education and healthcare were in a shambles; political repression was rife and nobody dared to utter a word of dissent; the country became isolated and was shunned; and foreign visitors were allowed only a twenty-four-hour visa, which was later extended.

When elections were announced for 2010, forty parties registered. Twenty-two of these were ethnic based; the rest

229

were political parties per se. The main opposition embodied by the National League for Democracy (NLD) and led by Daw Aung San Suu Kyi decided to boycott the elections on the grounds of inadequate election laws. There were, however, members of the NLD who felt it imperative to contest and form breakaway parties. They, in fact, succeeded in the elections and were elected to parliament. It was touching in a way, the excitement and elation we ordinary citizens felt that early morning as we walked to the election station at a nearby school on 7 November 2010.

Parliament met for the first time in December 2010 with 440 members in the Pyithu Hluttaw (House of Representatives) and 224 in the Amyotha Hluttaw (House of Nationalities). The USDP, led by the president-elect, won the majority of the seats in both houses. Reuters estimated that at least six other parties entering the elections were allied to the winning party. Added to that fact was the unpalatable and heavy presence of military appointees in each house. The National Democratic Force (NDF), formed by former members of the NLD, won eight seats in the Representatives and four in the Nationalities.

In December 2011, the NLD was re-registered for the first by-elections and had candidates contesting in forty-four out of the forty-six constituencies. The NLD leader, Daw Aung San Suu Kyi, stood for the constituency of Kawhmu in the Ayerwaddy Division. She and all but one NLD candidate were returned in those by-elections, meaning that now the party was represented by thirty-nine of its members in the Pyithu Hluttaw and by five in the Amyothar Hluttaw.

The year 2012 was a landmark year for Myanmar as far as international recognition and acceptance are concerned. Myanmar was very much in the world news, and its interaction with the outside world was taken to a whole new level. Myanmar was no longer a pariah nation, as Western media often described it. World leaders came, even if not on state visits, to stop by to congratulate Daw Aung San Su Kyi and the people. Chief among these visits was that of President Barack Obama of the United States of America, who gave a historic speech at the Convocation Hall of the University of

Yangon to the youth of Myanmar. This was preceded by the visits of former heads of states of Britain and Australia, and US Secretary of State Hillary Clinton. The prime minister of Sweden, and European Commission President José Barroso, met with Myanmar President U Thein Sein. Since then, U Thein Sein has visited the US White House (in May 2013). He was the first Myanmar president to visit the US White House in forty-seven years.

Some countries re-established diplomatic relations or upgraded their presence. The Royal Norwegian Embassy opened in October 2013, marking the increased bilateral relations and cooperation between the two countries. The European Union opened its representative office in Yangon, and US diplomatic representation resumed at an ambassadorial level after twelve years when Derek Mitchell presented his credentials to President U Thein Sein in Nay Pyi Taw in June 2012.

President U Thein Sein of Myanmar gave an address at the opening session of the 67th United Nations General Assembly meeting in New York, the first time in fifty years that a Myanmar head of state had addressed that meeting (U Nu last spoke in 1962). The president spoke candidly of the democratic reforms in his country, of the difficult road ahead, and of his hopes for the cooperation and support of the member states of the United Nations. He also expressed his admiration of the strength of purpose of the opposition leader Daw Aung Suu Kyi, in a first-ever public recognition of the Nobel Peace Prize winner and democracy activist.

Also in 2012, members of the Association of Southeast Asian Nations (ASEAN) agreed to Myanmar's chairmanship of the community. The country was chosen to host the ASEAN summit in 2014. In addition, the 27th SEA Games were held in Myanmar in December 2013 with commendable success.

At the same time, Myanmar's economy was starting to ferment, as a leavening agent was added to the mix with the prospect of foreign direct investments. The United States announced the suspension of sanctions of US investment in Myanmar. The European Union lifted all sanctions except for an arms embargo. Australia lifted remaining financial and travel restrictions. Myanmar was allowed debt relief to the amount of $6 billion from the Paris Club of creditor nations after Obama's visit. And the World Bank announced it would resume lending to Myanmar for the first time in more than two decades, focusing on poverty reduction. On its part, the Myanmar government implemented the new Foreign Investment Law to replace the existing 1988 version, allowing foreign investors up to an 80 per cent share in ventures in eleven restricted sectors. The Central Bank of Myanmar Law, enacted by parliament in July 2013, allowed the Central Bank more autonomy to implement its pivotal role in the country's economy in a timely manner. One of the key economic policy developments was the unification of the foreign exchange rate and the introduction of a managed float for the kyat. Private banks were allowed to accept foreign currency accounts and open currency exchange counters.

Opportunities for economic dealings with Myanmar were discussed in countries far and wide. The World Economic Forum on East Asia 2013 was held in Nay Pyi Taw and was attended by twelve hundred participants including ten heads of state, twelve ministers, and forty senior directors from all over the world. The Norway–Asia Business Summit in April 2014 brought forty representatives from Norwegian companies. Meetings were held in Bangkok on the topic of economic development and multi-lateral trade relations. Many less visible tentacles were reached out to private Myanmar nationals who had aspirations of doing business with foreign partners.

Some significant changes had been made in the sphere of human rights, although not all political prisoners had been freed. Dissidents abroad had been taken off the blacklist and were allowed to visit or settle back home. They have become active in such organizations as the Myanmar Peace Centre, which openly works for negotiations and agreements with opposition national groups. Youths of the 1988 generation who had fled the country after the uprising and subsequent crackdown and who had lived in exile returned to form political parties such as the 88 Generation Party. These people are now actively engaged in reform initiatives. Still, there remain unresolved thorny issues, which are seen as gaping holes in the government's human-rights record.

Freedom-of-the-press activists speak to foreign media about their disappointments and disenchantment with the so-called liberalization policies. They openly voice their dissatisfaction over the paucity of information fed to the public by government departments. There also remain serious misgivings of how "free" the press could actually be. However that may be, many books published in the West and locally that would never have been allowed into the country before are now visible on the shelves. There are more than a dozen dailies and weeklies with names like *Seven Day, Shwe Myanmar, Daily Eleven, The Voice,* and the *Myanmar Times* beside the government's own publications. These all do their part to bring issues or cases to the public's attention when transparency is in short supply. At the same time, the issue of media ethics has not escaped scrutiny.

There is a plethora of glossies on fashion, style, and lifestyle advertising anything from beauty products to vitamins. Models strut the runway for any of a number of causes, such as to honour the successful hosting of the SEA Games in Myanmar, to commemorate Myanmar Women's Day, and to launch dozens of products. Myanmar beauties were selected to compete in international beauty pageants such as Miss Universe and Miss World.

In January 2014, Norway's Telenor and Qatar's Ooredoo, two telecoms giants, won Myanmar's telecom licences to make telecommunications and the Internet more accessible to, and cheaper for, millions of the country's residents. Myanmar Posts and Telegraphs (MPT), which previously held the monopoly, has now joined forces with Japan to remain competitive in the field.

Travel outside of the country is free and easy now, no longer the hassle it used to be. Extensive documentation and lengthy processing time has been replaced by a system allowing passports to be issued within ten working days. What would seem commonplace to other country nationals were for us in the recent past problems to be surmounted, if one had the will. Now countries like Brunei, Laos, Cambodia, the Philippines, Vietnam, and Indonesia have signed visa exemption agreements, and more ASEAN countries are expected to follow suit. Five domestic carriers and twenty international airlines operate out of a modernized and expanded Yangon International Airport, which is the oldest airport in the country but only the third largest, after the Nay Pyi Taw International Airport and Mandalay International Airport. The much-vaunted international airport in Hanthawaddy, slated to be the biggest in Myanmar, is still battling administrative hitches.

Transactions in foreign currencies are no longer a crime punishable by jail sentence. Citizens can own foreign currency accounts. Currency exchange counters abound in hotels, supermarkets, and licensed offices everywhere. With the influx of foreign companies and a foreign workforce from the highest echelons of business down to skilled labourers, salaries and rent are now habitually paid in US dollars.

Tourism has received a huge boost. From being rated among the best places to travel in 2014 by *Travel + Leisure* magazine to hosting the ASEAN summit in December 2014, Myanmar has been gearing up to meet the demand for hotel accommodation, transport, and banking facilities, and skilled personnel in all sectors.

The fact that Myanmar also became part of the ASEAN Economic Community (AEC) in 2015 means there is a dire need for our workforce to upgrade in all respects in order to be competitive as well as to enable workers to meet the demands of an international business community, which we are hoping to attract. Inasmuch as improvements are seen to be insurmountable in this regard, at least in the short term, there is evidence of a committed and determined youth force which has read the signs and is putting in every effort to prepare itself by gaining experience abroad, pursuing further qualifications, and attending workshops and seminars. Indeed, many ASEAN countries as well as others like Japan and Germany are contributing resources to this end. Statistics from the World Economic Forum show that Myanmar's working-age population has increased over the last ten years and is projected to increase. With a median age of twenty-seven, this factor is considered one of the attractive features of investing in Myanmar. However, this optimism is only justifiable if education and skills are upgraded comprehensively for this emerging resource.

The public educational sector, underfunded, neglected, experimented with, and bungled, is now receiving nationwide attention. The National Education Seminar, recently held in Nay Pyi Taw, was attended by ministers and high-ranking officials of the Ministry of Education, foreign educationists, and teachers. The non-governmental reform committee calling itself the National Network for Educational Reform (NNER) and consisting of university professors, lecturers, and students was not invited to attend. The NLD's Education Network, however, won the Myanmar Citizen Award from a civil award committee formed in 2010 by overseas Myanmar families. Both the NNER and the Education Network have rejected a new bill, approved by parliament in July 2014, which calls for the formation of a national Education Committee and a Higher Education Coordination Committee. Their rejection is based on the grounds that autonomy for universities and higher-education institutions has not been assured under the terms of this bill, which instead would preserve central government control of education.

I feel sure that a country that had been in hibernation for the better part of a century, while the rest of the region had leapt into the twenty-first, is bound to have a lot of catching up to do in numerous aspects, especially social and economic. Thus while we can see progress in some fields, there are many that have sadly lagged behind. In these wholly or partially neglected areas, there have arisen many non-governmental community-based organizations which have taken up the challenge and achieved commendable success and recognition. But, in fact, their existence serves to glaringly show up the inadequacy of the government apparatus.

The single most eventful phenomenon, however, is the return of the "natives" from all over the world. Repatriates, as they are termed, are young mid-career professionals who were educated and trained abroad, such as in the United Kingdom, the United States, Canada, Australia, and Singapore, and who have been inspired to return to work and earn a living back in their home country. They wished to return for a number of personal reasons. There are also retirees with a broad range of professional expertise and experience from eminent positions in international organizations who feel a compelling need to contribute to the restructuring and reconstruction of their country. There is an initial sense of excitement and enthusiasm as they envision the improvements they could help make for their country.

With this momentous change in the backdrop of Myanmar's economic and political scene, my own family and many others like it are going through scenarios which they had never before expected to experience. Both my son and daughter are back in the country after more than a decade of foreign business experience. Their expertise is needed and useful in a newly emerging economy. The same goes for many of their peers who have found that their knowledge and exposure to international business practices and norms could be advantageously put to use to provide momentum for the economic resurgence in the country. It is, in fact, a win-win situation when young Myanmar nationals with sound education and adequate work experience successfully engage with expatriates and their compatriots on native ground and abroad.

On a personal level, my husband and I, like many other aged parents, are benefiting from the presence of our children and grandchildren, who undeniably brighten up our lives. If they also undeniably complicate what would otherwise be placid lives, that could be placed squarely at the doors of phenomena known as the "generation gap" and "technological advances." In our young working lives, our parents could freely make comments to us, advise us, and guide us, as the terms of reference in the workplace were familiar to them. The workplace culture, traditions, and constraints were very similar, as we all mostly worked for government departments, be it in education, public works, or public services. Not so for us with our children. Their professional lives are way out of our ken. They work for themselves in new fields like software architecture and multimedia, or for big multinational organizations. They travel, they work across time zones, they network, and they bear tremendous pressure. Quite simply put, they inhabit a wider world, physically and metaphorically, than we ourselves did at their ages.

As a grandmother, I held it as my inalienable right to pamper my grandchildren in a way I did not get to do with my own children, for lack of money and time. But alas, I express this in the past tense, as I ought, since it is not to be. When they were young enough for me to have the opportunity, my grandchildren lived abroad. I visited as frequently as I could, but what chance does a visiting grandmother have but to get into a regimen already set in the household? If I dared to make a change, the little toddler was sure to look at me strangely and tell me, "This is not how Mummy does it." Now that my grandchildren are with me, they are a little grown up and they are busy. They have so many activities: play practice, school group projects, third language classes, martial arts, and travel. I do not even mention the scourge of the young generation, the Internet and Internet games, because my grandchildren are restricted in that regard.

Be that as it may, I live now a charmed life, one wherein I am fulfilled and attended to by my children as much as their professional and social lives allow. I enjoy the company of my siblings Htut and Moe and my sister-in-law Ju Ju, who have moved back to Myanmar, and Polay and his wife, Ta Ta. We celebrate birthdays, anniversaries, and reunions; observe special religious days with a *soon kyway* for the monks; and travel, within and outside of Myanmar, for shared enjoyment and to visit members of the extended families who are still scattered abroad. I was blessed with another grandson, Zahni, born to Wai Sann Thi and Cameron in January 2010. Polay and Ta Ta became grandparents when Mon Thiri and Jin gave birth to Kai Thura in October 2011. They welcomed Wyn Oung Soe Lin into their family when Amara married him in February 2012. Wyn is the son of Soe Lin and Mya Darli, and the grandson of

Aunty Sally, a family friend who goes back generations to our Kyimyindine roots.

The diaspora that I spoke about has taken the descendants of U Tha Myaing and Daw Aye Myaing across four continents, five countries, and more than ten cities of the world. The third, fourth, and fifth generations are almost equally divided between the group that settled in Myanmar and the group that had scattered. But in what could be described as an unexpected scenario, many of those living abroad have returned, the young and the old. They or their parents had gone to seek greener pastures to escape from what had been an untenable situation within their home country. They had gone unwillingly and always wished to return if situations improved. Some, on the other hand, had taken to living in their new, adopted countries like a duck to water. They would say, on various counts, that coming back home, except on visits, would not work. No prejudice is attached to either choice.

In this world that we live in, the "global village," distances have shrunk: Cameron will come to pick up Zahni on a weekend for his twice annual visits to Perth; Tin Aung Myaing and Jennifer flew from New Jersey for a two-week stay to supervise the building of their family home on Inya Road; and Mon Thiri and her son Kai came for a lightning visit from Tokyo while Jin travelled to Seattle on business. Bangkok and Singapore are to Aung Thura extensions of his own home, as the Myanmar saying goes, for not a month goes by that he does not travel out on business. The Internet and social media keep each one of us who is willing to be so involved in a constant barrage of activities and moods at any time when anyone wants to share.

Values have changed. It is no wonder. Values have changed within the generations and among people who have lived or grown up in different cultures. I would accept value changes in my children while at the same time insisting that the fundamental values of human decency and dignity prevail. I would even venture to say that the young these days are even more aware than we were of their responsibility as citizens of the world they live in, with all the ramifications that it implies. But one thing is fundamental. I believe that we should all know who we are and where we came from.

All that is gold does not glitter,
Not all those who wander are lost;
The old that is strong does not wither,
Deep roots are not reached by the frost.

—J. R. R. Tolkien, *The Fellowship of the Ring*

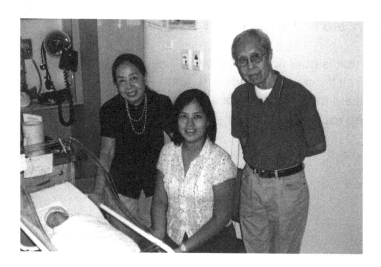

Zahni lies in a cot as Grandfather U Soe Myint and
Grandmother visit him in hospital, January 2010

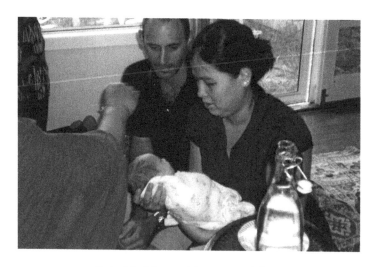

Zahni is blessed by a monk in a
Kinpuntat ceremony, March 2010

Mon Thiri and Kai Thura relaxing in a Tokyo park

Amara Thiri Myaing and Wyn Oung Soe Lin
at their wedding ceremony, February 2012

A Note on Sources

For information on the insurrections in Chapter 2, I have relied almost entirely on Bohmugyi Tin Maung's (retd) book (in Myanmar language) *Taing pyay ka nu nu, mon htine ka htan htan,* although other works have been used as cross reference, as well as oral history from people who lived and fought through that period in history.

The quotation I made in the first chapter is a non-literal translation I had made of the end note of Bogyoke Aung San's last public speech, delivered at the People's Assmebly, at the Town Hall in Yangon, six days before his assassination on July 19 1947.

To refresh my memory of the many enjoyable times and activities at MEHS, I found the collected memoirs of friends and alumni of the school, published and distributed at the 2014 international MEHSA reunion in Yangon, to be a big help. Thanks are due to Tommy Htay and Cecil Teoh, the latter my classmate, who were chief among the movers and shakers for that MEHS publication.

It was very difficult to find anyone who could recount the day's events on the actual day Burma celebrated its independence from Britain, on 4 January 1948. U Kyaw Thein Lwin, who is married to my cousin Khin Saw Thwin (Saw Saw), was able to supply me with interesting details of the contributions he made to the day's celebrations. His book *The Gun That Saved Rangoon* is the one I quote in Chapter 2.

As for the historically important pictures of the ceremony that took place in New Delhi, my sister-in-law Thein Thein Nwe very generously brought out the photo collection of her mother, Daw Khin Khin Maw, and made those pictures available to me. Daw Khin Khin Maw was a great collector in her time. While the rest of the family complained often of the masses of books and literature she had piled on every available tabletop and spare bed, these proved valuable in time. Many were the people who coveted parts of that collection.

Daw Khin Khin Maw had also related to her daughter how her husband, U Hla Aung, as a young third secretary was sent ahead by sea with other staff to open up the Burmese Embassy in New Delhi in 1947. They were charged with making preparations for the auspicious event, which the newly appointed ambassador H. E. U Win was to host on 4 January 1948.

The rest of the story is based on my own recollections prompted by the many pictures I have in my collection of friends and family, often faded and torn since they have not been digitized. Some, however, were supplied by my brothers at my request to make more engaging, and provide relevant imagery for, the events in our shared journey.

Appendix I:
Coda

Wai Wai Myaing retired in May 2014 after forty-seven years of service in the education sector, her last position being that of an administrator at a small international school.

Htin Myaing, an architect by profession, has returned to Myanmar from New Jersey, USA, and is engaged as an urban planning consultant with the Asian Development Bank.

Kyaw Myaing, a retired diplomat, has returned to Myanmar from New Jersey, USA, and is the managing director of Ayezay Aungzay Economic Enterprise Co. Ltd. He is involved in development of the education sector and of trade ties between Myanmar and the United States.

Linn Myaing retired from the Foreign Service in 2006 and is presently working in the private sector as the executive director of First Myanmar Investment Co. Ltd. (FMI).

Aung Thura (BBA, Hawaii Pacific University) is chief strategist of his own media company, Ignite Marketing Communications, and co-founder of the Professional Marketers' Association.

Tin Aung Myaing (BSc, City University of New York) is a designer, developer, and entrepreneur who creates gamified software for schools, museums, and the government. He lives in Manhattan.

Myo Htut Myaing (BSc, City College of New York; M.Arch., School of Architecture and Environmental Studies, CUNY), former resident of New Jersey, USA, and author of *Think Richly* is currently working in project management at Serge Pun Associates (SPA). He lives in Star City, Than Lyin.

Mon Thiri Myaing (BSc, Bryn Mawr; PhD, University of Michigan) is the full-time mother of her son, Kai Thura, with whom she and her husband live in Tokyo.

Wai Sann Thi (BBA, Baruch College, CUNY; MBA, University of Western Australia) last worked as an associate at the representative office of Australia New Zealand (ANZ) Bank in Myanmar, one of nine leading foreign banks awarded a licence to operate in the country. She now lives in Western Australia.

Amara Thiri Myaing (Masters in Earth Environmental Resource Management (MEERM), University of South Carolina) works for the International Monetary Fund and lives in Bethesda, Maryland, USA.

Tun Htut Myaing (MFA, New York Academy of Art; BFA, Fashion Institute of Technology) is an artist whose work is widely shown in New York and exists in private collections. He is the curator of many successful group shows and the director of the project space Art Foundry US. He lives and works in Queens, New York.

Chan Myay Eindre Myaing is now a freshman in high school at the International School of Myanmar (ISM). Art and history are her favourite subjects. She played Rapunzel in ISM's production of *The Brothers Grimm Spectaculathon.*

Nay Thurein Aung is in year three at the International School of Myanmar. He is a green belt in karate and is a big Chelsea Football Club fan.

Zahni Kingston Russell was in Foundation 2 at the Network International School and loved to keep his *pwa pwa* (grandmother) informed of the names of various dinosaurs and of creatures of the deep, including those that inhabit the Mariana Trench. He now attends Grovelands Primary School in Perth, Australia, and goes to Helen O'Grady Drama Academy.

Kai Thura Yamamoto goes to day care at Mahou no Hoikuen in Tokyo and is passionate about Thomas the Tank Engine.

Miya Thiri Yamamoto, a sister for Kai, was very warmly welcomed into the family on August 15, 2015, just in time to be included in the family chronology.

Appendix II:
Who's Who in *Of Roots and Wings*

Aung San, Bogyoke	Martyred independence leader and prime minister in the cabinet of the Union of Burma before his assassination in July 1947.
Aung San Suu Kyi	Daughter of Bogyoke Aung San and democracy activist. Nobel Peace Prize winner and leader of the opposition National League for Democracy Party. Parliamentary delegate for the Kawmhu constituency.
Aye Hlaing	PhD; head of economics department (1957–64), University of Rangoon; rector (1964–75), Institute of Economics; advisor, Ministry of Planning.
Bigandet, Monsignor	First Catholic bishop of Lower and Upper Burma (Court of Ava), in 1856. Wrote *The Life or Legend of Gaudama* (1858).
Chit Hlaing	Research officer in the Directorate of Psychological Warfare and the brains behind *The System of the Correlation of Man and His Environment* (1963), which became the philosophy of the Burma Socialist Programme Party.

Fend, Than E	Aka Dora Than Aye, by which name she was famous as a singer; subsequently with the United Nations Information Agency.
Goh, Daw Shwe	Aunt and stepmother to the children of U Tha Myaing.
Hla Aung	Head of division, Ministry of Foreign Affairs; chief of reparations, Myanmar Embassy, Tokyo
Htut Saing	Aka Harry; FRCS, FAAP, FHKCPS; emeritus professor of paediatric surgery. Performed jointly with Dr Pe Thein a medical procedure to separate congenitally joined twins for the first time in Myanmar.
Htwe Maung	Sixth son of U Tha Myaing; chief accountant of Municipal Corporation; head scout in Burma Scouts Federation.
Khin Aye Pwint	Aka Anna, née Kyaw Nyunt; MA (English); lecturer in English and author of several books on spoken and written English.
Khin Aye Win,	DLitt; aka Elsie; youngest daughter of U Po Sa; professor, Department of Psychology, University of Yangon.
Khin Maung Bo	Eldest son of U Tin; commander-in-chief of the Burma navy; commanding officer of SS *Mayu* at the time the British government handed over the vessel to what was to be newly independent Burma.

Khin Maung Kyi — PhD (Cornell), MBA (Harvard); professor, Research Department, Institute of Economics (1954–78); author of *Economic Development of Burma: A Vision and a Strategy,* 2001; senior fellow of the National University of Singapore, Department of Business Policy, 1991.

Khin Maung Nyunt — PhD (London School of Economics); rector (1977–93), Institute of Economics.

Khin Maung Yin — Renowned artist and architect; grandson of Sithu U Tin.

Khin Thet Tin, Daw — Wife of Sithu U Tin; prominent Myanmar architect and engineer best known for designing the iconic Yangon City Hall and Yangon Central Railway Station.

Khin Win Kyi — Aka Sheila neé Saing; English lecturer at Assumption Business Administration College (ABAC) University, Bangkok, Thailand.

Kyaw Thein Lwin — Si Thu Consecutively, commander of gunboat in the Burma Royal Naval Volunteer Reserve; harbour master at the Port of Rangoon; marine superintendent of Burma Five Star Line; principal of Institute of Marine Academy; author of *The Gun That Saved Rangoon.*

Kyaw Win, Brig. Gen. — Fellow of the Royal College of Physicians (FRCP); director of medical services, Burma Army Medical Corps; author of *Textbook of Internal Medicine* and of numerous international publications on malaria and problems with its treatment; retired Myanmar ambassador to Canada and the Court of St James.

Kyi Kyi Khine — Ophthalmologist resident, Royal Eye Hospital, Surbiton, England.

Kyi Kyi Kyaw Win	B.Com.; daughter of U Chit Maung (president of Myanmar Nylon Industry and pioneering manufacturer of Rachel Laces in South East Asia in the 1950s); advocate; wife of Brig. Gen. Kyaw Win.
Ma Ma Gyi	MA (Burmese); wife of U Tun Ohn; student activist; commissioner of Municipal Corporation.
McLennan, Margaret	Fellow student at the London School of Economics.
Mi Mi Khaing	Scholar and writer; author of *Burmese Family* (Bloomington: Indiana University Press, 1962), *Cook and Entertain the Burmese Way* (Karoma Publishers, 1978), and *The World of Burmese Women* (London: Zed Press, 1984).
Mya Baw	Son of Daw Mya Sein and U Shwe Baw; married to cousin (Than Than Nwe) Betty née Tin Maung.
Mya Sein, Daw	Daughter of U May Oung; MA, Oxford University; delegate to the Round Table Conference; lecturer, history department, University of Rangoon.
Mya Soe Sint	Aka Shirley; FRCS; daughter of U Bo (Imperial Police Service, inspector general of police)
Mya Thanda	Aka Helen; daughter of Daw Mya Sein and U Shwe Baw; head of Asian Division, Library of Congress, 2000.
Myo Khaing	Ophthalmologist; son of Justice U Aung Khine.
Naw Seng	Anti-Japanese war hero and leader of Kachin rebel forces during civil war.

Nu, U	First prime minister of a freely elected government in independent Burma. Author of *Saturday's Son* and *Burma under the Japanese.*
Nu Nu, Daw	Eldest daughter of U Tin and wife of U Htwe Maung; teacher at MEHS.
Ohn Ghine	PhD; professor of history, Rangoon University.
Pain, A. C. D.	British gems merchant stationed in Mogok in 1948.
Paw, William	MBA (Harvard); head of economics department (1951–53), University of Rangoon; professor and head of Commerce Department (1964–77), Institute of Economics.
Pe Maung	Superintendent of land records; father of Patrick, Patricia, and Patterson.
Pe Maung Tin	PhD; Pali professor; principal of University College, Rangoon University (1937); president of the Burma Research Society (1939 and 1950); chairman of the Burma Historical Commission (1960–64); prodigious writer.
Rance, Sir Hubert	Major General Sir Hubert Elvin Rance, last British governor of colonial Burma (1946–48).
Raschid, U	Student activist in the Independence movement together with Bogyoke Aung San; minister of labour in U Nu's cabinet.
Sao Saimong Mangrai	Scholar, historian, and linguist; author of *The Shan States and the British Annexation* (Cornell: Cornell University Press, 1965; 2nd ed. 1969) and *The Padaeng Chronicle and the Jengtung State Chronicle Translated* (Ann Arbor: University of Michigan Press, 1981).

Sao Shwe Thaike	Shan *sawbwa* (chief) and first president of independent Burma.
Shwe Shane	General manager of Burma Railways and subsequently of ESCAP, Bangkok.
Soe Soe, Daw	Aka Sally; youngest daughter of Sithu U Tin; wife of U San Lin; general manager of Central Bank of Myanmar and, subsequently, of the International Monetary Fund.
Tha Hto	Professor and head of the Economics Department (1964–80), Institute of Economics.
Tha Myaing	The first Myanmar to be accepted into the Imperial Forest Service, *Kyetthayay Saungya Min* (KSM), *Ahmhu Tan Kaung Min* (ATM), my grandfather (1867–1926).
Tha Sin	Chief engineer, Burma Railways.
Thakin Soe	Leader of the White Flag Communist Party.
Than Aung	Son of U Aung Chein; MBBS, DO (London); FRCS (Edin); professor and head of ophthalmology department, Institute of Medicine.
Than Tun, Thakin	Leader of the Red Flag Communist Party.
Than Tun,	PhD; professor of history, Rangoon University.
Thant, U	Secretary to Prime Minister U Nu (1951–57); permanent representative to the United Nations (1957–61); UN secretary general (1961–71).

Thaw Kaung	Chief librarian, Universities Central Library; professor, head of department, library and information studies, Rangoon Arts and Science University; honorary Doctor of Letters, University of Western Sydney, Australia; Academic Prize laureate at the Fukuoka Asian Culture Prizes, 2005; author of Tun Foundation Literary Award–winning books *From the Librarian's Window* (2009) and *Glimpses of Myanmar History and Culture* (2010).
Thein Nyunt	Chief accountant, Burma Railways.
Thein Yin	Fourth son of U Tha Myaing; divisional forest officer.
Thet Su, U and Mrs	FAO in Rome; chairman of the 1953 FAO Conference in Rome.
Tin, Jimmy	Architect; graduated from Harvard University; youngest son of Sithu U Tin; resides in the United States.
Tin Maung	Fifth son of U Tha Myaing; deputy permanent representative to the United Nations under U Thant; president of the UN Trusteeship Council (1961).
Tin Tin Myaing	Aka Brenda; youngest daughter of Dr Pe Maung Tin; scholar of French language and literature; librarian; lives in London.
Tin Tin Nwe	Aka Shirley; B.Com., University of Rangoon; married to Alwyn Bwa; resides in California, USA.
Tin Tun, Lt. General	Maha Thray Sithu; air chief marshal; deputy prime minister, State Law and Order Restoration Council, Myanmar.

Trevelyan, Mary	CBE; founder and governor of International Students House, London, and founder of the Goats Club for foreign students, a weekly intercollegiate gathering of international students.
Tun Aung	Son of U Aung Chein; Burmese section, Voice of America; resides in Virginia.
Tun Ohn	Student activist and member of University Students' Union in the 1930s. Commissioner of Municipal Corporation.
Tun Thein	Director of Cottage Industries and subsequently with ESCAP, Bangkok.
Win Pe	ICS, Maha Thray Sithu, chief secretary; Myanmar's ambassador to Italy in 1971.

Appendix III: Glossary

ahlu an act of dhana, by providing food and drink for monks and or other invited guests, aimed at gaining merit.

ahlushin host of the alhu; the person who is giving the feast or making the donation.

anyeint pwe a traditional performance featuring dancers accompanied by a music ensemble and comedians, usually performed at night on open-air stages.

Ao dai traditional dress or costume that Vietnamese women wear.

Areimedeya the name of the fifth Buddha that will arise.

Asi Asin programme, agenda.

Badda Kabar Buddhist concept of the universe proposing that five Buddhas will arise, Gautama being the fourth and Areimedeya being the fifth and last in the Badda Kabar.

balachaung a spicy condiment of fried dried prawns with garlic and onions.

baw a type of silver mined in the Shan states.

Bikkhu senior monk.

Bohshu Khan Mandat a pavilion from which a head of state or a head of the military views a ceremonial parade.

buthikyaw fritters of gourd.

cetana generosity; wishing well for others.

dhana the act of giving.

dobat-waing a music ensemble featuring drums, flute, and bamboo clappers.

htamane pwe a communal preparation of sticky rice, coconut, peanuts and sesame seed, often staged as a community event. The objective is to offer this to Buddha on the fullmoon day of *Tabodwe*.

Janekha a prince in one of the lives of the Buddha.

Jataka tales of the five hundred lives of Gautama before gaining enlightenment.

kadaw pyitsi offerings of food and consumables for people to whom you pay homage.

kathakali traditional dance drama of Kerala, India.

keema paratha paratha stuffed with a spicy meat mixture.

ker lar a type of window which has a flap that is pushed up with a stave to stay open.

kimpun acacia soap used to wash hair.

Ko Ko elder brother, to refer to an older male.

koyin a novice monk.

kut pyit a raised seating area made of wood.

kyaukpyin a stone implement on which thanakha is ground to get a paste.

kyaukyaw a dessert made from agar-agar and coconut milk.

Kyee Kyee elder aunt

laphet pickled tea leaves usually eaten with an accompaniment of fried beans, fried garlic, and sesame seeds.

longyi a garment traditionally worn by Myanmar women tied around the waist, and of various colours and designs.

Ma Ma elder sister, to refer to an older female.

mandat a temporary structure for accommodating a large number of people.

mhaw sayar an exorcist.

mohinga a Myanmar noodle dish with a fish-based soup.

mont lon yay baw floating rice balls with jaggery filling.

Mya Pan Ghway title of a song first made famous by Bilat Pyan Than, or Daw Than Aye.

ngapi-yay extract of fermented fish or prawns.

ohno kaukswe a Myanmar noodle dish with chicken in a coconut-milk soup.

ossasaunt guardian spirits of treasure troves intended for the coming of the next Buddha.

padein-ngo name given to a flower of delicate yellow tendrils that usually grows wild in the wet season.

PaPaKa acronym for "People's Stores" during the socialist era.

paratha round, layered Indian bread cooked in oil.

parittas religious verses that are recited on various occasions.

pasoe garment worn by Myanmar men in place of trousers, tied around the waist and usually patterned with checks and stripes.

Phan Khon a traditional game for young girls which involves jumping over the stacked feet and hands of the opposing team member.

Pho Pho Grandfather.

pwe a celebration of any kind.

Pyithu Hluttaw legislative body of the people.

saing waing a Myanmar music ensemble of drums, flute, and xylophone.

samanera novice monk.

sanwinmakin a pudding made of semolina and coconut milk.

satudithar a feast that needs no invitation where everyone who comes is fed.

sawbwa Shan for chieftain.

Sayardaw senior monk or abbot.

shinpyu a ceremony where young Burmese Buddhist boys are initiated into the monkhood.

shwe yin aye concoction of coconut milk with sago, agar-agar, and sticky rice served on ice.

Shwe Yo main character from a rustic Myanmar dance routine.

sin tu to look alike.

si-sar-oke literally, the oil-quota book, issued for each household listing the members and their genders, ages, and occupations, the basis on which essential commodities were allotted during the socialist era.

sone a witch.

soon offering of a meal for the monks.

soon kyway a meal offered to the monks either at dawn or before noon. Usually friends and family are also invited to share in the dhana and the meal.

Taw Ein a village dwelling; a hut.

tayaw bark of a vine used to wash hair.

Tazaungdine a festival of lights occurring on the full-moon day of the month of Tazaungmon.

Thadingyut a festival of lights occurring on the full-moon day of the month of Thadingyut, also signifying the end of the Buddhist Lent.

thagu tapioca, or a dessert made from tapioca.

thanakha a paste made from the bark of the thanakha tree worn as a cosmetic by Myanmar women both for aesthetic and therapeutic qualities.

Thingyan a water festival preceding the Myanmar New Year.

Upoke observation of the Buddhist precepts.

Vesandara, King one of the incarnations of the Buddha.

zartar a horoscope written on palm leaf, made traditionally for all newborn babies.

zat traditional performance usually on outdoor stage, featuring dance, drama, and song.

zayat a place of rest for weary travellers or a house in religious precincts for use by laypeople for religious purpose.

Note*: Ko, Ma, U,* and *Daw* are honorifics applying to Myanmar males and females relative to their age and station in life.

Appendix IV: Genealogy Tables

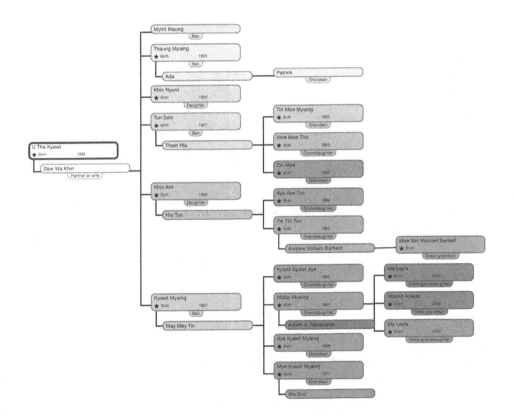

Descendant chart of U Tha Kyawt

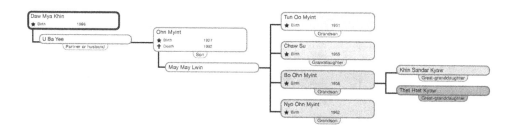

Descendant chart of Daw Mya Khin

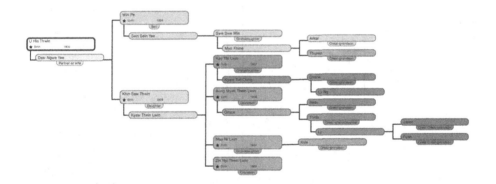

Descendant chart of U Hla Thwin

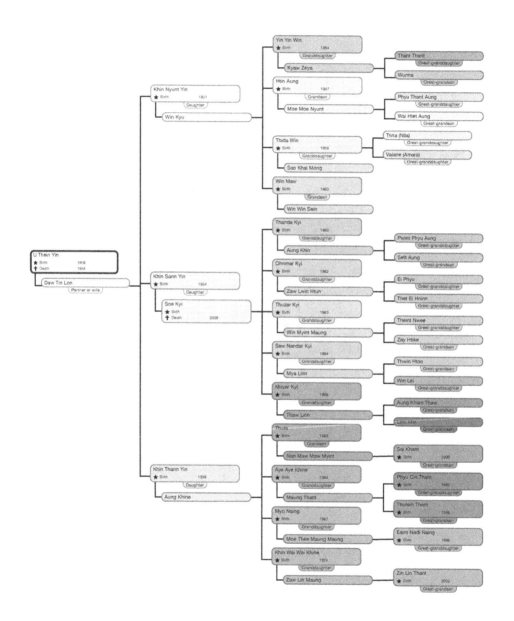

Descendant chart of U Thein Yin

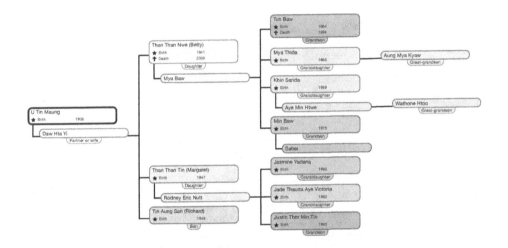

Descendant chart of U Tin Maung

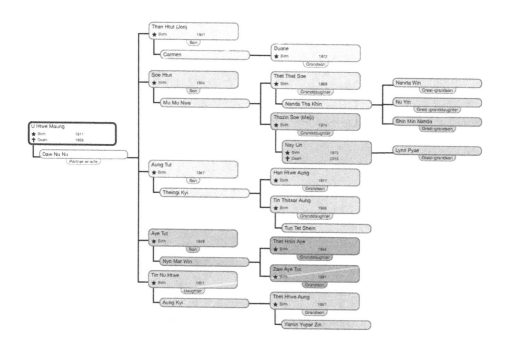

Descendant chart of U Htwe Maung

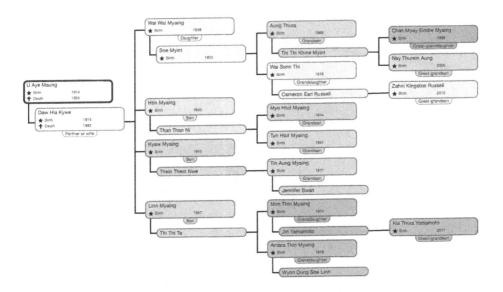

Descendant chart of U Aye Maung

Printed in the United States
By Bookmasters